M000288574

JAPANESE in 7

KIMIKO BARBER is a Japanese cook and demonstrator who teaches regularly at cookery schools around the UK. She is the author of *The Japanese Kitchen*, *The Chopsticks Diet* and *Japanese Pure and Simple*, which was shortlisted for the World Food Media and Guild of Food Writers' healthy eating awards, and *Cook Japanese at Home*. Her books have been translated into German, Spanish and Polish. Kimiko divides her time between London and Oxfordshire where she grows vegetables and keeps honeybees.

www.kimikobarber.co.uk   @kimiko_barber

JAPANESE in 7

DELICIOUS JAPANESE RECIPES IN **7** INGREDIENTS OR FEWER

KIMIKO BARBER

PHOTOGRAPHY BY EMMA LEE

KYLE BOOKS

An Hachette UK Company
www.hachette.co.uk

First published as part of *Cook Japanese at Home* in 2016
This edition first published in Great Britain in 2020 by
Kyle Books, an imprint of Kyle Cathie Ltd
Carmelite House
50 Victoria Embankment
London EC4Y 0DZ
www.kylebooks.co.uk

ISBN: 978 085783 844 5

Text copyright 2016 © Kimiko Barber
Design and layout copyright 2020 © Kyle Cathie Ltd
Photography copyright 2016 © Emma Lee

Distributed in the US by Hachette Book Group, 1290 Avenue of the Americas,
4th and 5th Floors, New York, NY 10104

Distributed in Canada by Canadian Manda Group, 664 Annette St., Toronto, Ontario, Canada M6S 2C8

Kimiko Barber is hereby identified as the author of this work in accordance with section 77 of the Copyright,
Designs and Patents Act 1988.

All rights reserved. No part of this work may be reproduced or utilised in any form or by any means, electronic
or mechanical, including photocopying, recording or by any information storage and retrieval system, without
the prior written permission of the publisher.

Publisher: Joanna Copestick
Editorial Director: Judith Hannam
Editor: Vicky Orchard
Editorial assistant: Sarah Kyle
Design: Georgia Vaux
Photography: Emma Lee
Food styling: Aya Nishimura
Props styling: Lucy Attwater
Production: Emily Noto

A Cataloguing in Publication record for this title is available from the British Library.

Printed and bound in China

10 9 8 7 6 5 4 3 2 1

NOTE
In this book where dashi is listed as an ingredient, it refers to primary dashi unless otherwise stated.

CONTENTS

INTRODUCTION

Over the past decade or so, Japanese cuisine has gained phenomenal international popularity. When I first arrived in England in the 1970s there were very few Japanese restaurants. Today, there are more than 200 in central London alone, many of which require booking days, if not weeks, in advance, and boxes of sushi are sold next to sandwiches in supermarkets.

The Japanese have one of the highest life expectancies in the world and, despite the fact that the traditional cuisine is widely recognized as a healthy choice, it is often still perceived as difficult to prepare. I want to show you just how easy it is to cook Japanese food at home any night of the week. There is no doubt that many classic Japanese recipes do call for a lot of ingredients and cannot be made without the entire list. I haven't included these recipes here, focusing instead on simple sushi, nourishing soups and comforting bowls of noodles and rice. If you have a reasonably well-equipped kitchen, you won't need any new equipment to make these dishes and one of the benefits of the ever-increasing popularity of Japanese cuisine is that the ingredients have also become much easier to find in supermarkets.

I have chosen three "cheat" basic ingredients, which form the cornerstone of many dishes alongside up to seven other ingredients. My cheats are: dashi, soy sauce/salt and cooking oil. Dashi is the stock that forms the foundation of much of Japanese cuisine. Dashi, unlike Western stock where simple ingredients are simmered for a long time, is instead a selection of carefully prepared ingredients that are briefly soaked in water or heated so as to extract nothing other than the very essence of the ingredients' flavour. In general, there are two types – *ichiban* (primary) dashi and *niban* (secondary) dashi. In this book where dashi is listed as an ingredient, it refers to primary dashi unless otherwise stated.

In Japanese cuisine, dashi provides a subtle undertone to almost all foods. It is not an overstatement to say that dashi is at the heart of Japanese cuisine, not because of the prominence of its own flavour, but because of the way it enhances and harmonises the flavours of other ingredients. So, you can understand why it had to be one of my "cheats". Before the age of instant seasonings, almost every Japanese meal began with making fresh dashi from scratch. Today, most Japanese home cooks rely on instant dashi, packaged granules that dissolve in hot water, generically called *dashi-no-moto*, and you probably will turn to this instant method also. Although some are excellent, nothing compares with the subtle flavour and delicate aroma of freshly made dashi. I believe it is important that you understand the traditional method, especially when it is neither difficult nor time consuming, so you can find my recipe on page 143.

Soy sauce is one of the most important primary seasoning ingredients in Japanese food. Made of fermented soya beans, wheat, salt and water. Outside Japan you will find dark and light soy sauce and tamari. Dark is the all-rounder used for both cooking and dipping while light is saltier and used only for cooking. Tamari is thicker and slightly sweeter and is used for dipping. It contains no wheat, which is thought to enhance the aroma. Although soy sauce keeps for a long time, it is best kept refrigerated or at least in a cool, dark place and used within a few months of opening.

Apart from these three key basic ingredients, each recipe uses seven additional ingredients or fewer (not including any serving suggestions or optional toppings given in the recipes, nor any water used/listed). This means shorter preparation and cooking times, so you can make a meal with minimum effort. The aim of this book is to make these recipes part of your weekly repertoire and to show you just how easy it is to put delicious Japanese food on your table in no time at all, using just a handful of ingredients.

FRESH

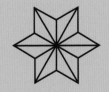

MUSHROOM SOBA [KINOKO SOBA]

Mushrooms are loved by Japanese people for their flavour, aroma and texture. In this dish, the broth is lightly thickened with cornflour to match the mushrooms' silky texture. You can use any mushrooms of your choice.

Serves 2

✻	✻	✻	✻	✻	✻	✻
4 shiitake mushrooms	50g (1¾oz) shimeji mushrooms	50g (1¾oz) enoki mushrooms	600ml (20fl oz) soup broth (300ml/½ pint All-purpose Noodle Sauce, *see* page 152, mixed with 300ml/½ pint water)	2 tablespoons cornflour mixed with 2 tablespoons cold water	200g (7oz) dried soba noodles	1 spring onion, finely chopped on the diagonal, to serve

Cut off and discard the stems of the shiitake mushrooms. Both shimeji and enoki mushrooms are joined at the base, so cut and discard the bases and separate the clumps into bite-sized clusters with your hands.

Put the mushrooms and the broth in a saucepan and heat until just below the boil, then stir in the cornflour mixture to thicken.

Meanwhile, cook the noodles as on page 164 and then portion between two warmed bowls. Ladle in the hot broth and arrange the mushrooms attractively, then scatter over the chopped spring onion and serve immediately.

YELLOWTAIL SASHIMI
[HAMACHI NO HIRAZUKURI]

Hirazukuri is a sashimi cut consisting of rectangular slices (about 1cm/½in thick). It is the most popular cutting technique and can be used for almost any type of fish.

Serves 4

❋	❋	❋	❋
5–7cm (2–2¾in) piece of daikon (giant white radish), peeled	250g (9oz) boneless and skinless yellowtail fillet	4 shiso, perilla leaves	4 teaspoons wasabi paste

With a mandoline, finely shred the radish and then soak the shreds in iced water for 20–30 minutes.

Place the fish fillet lengthways on a chopping board, former skin-side up, then cut into 1cm (½in) thick slices along the grain (you should have about 20 slices). Ideally, use a sashimi knife (*see page 171*). See how to cut rectangular slices below.

Drain the radish and divide into four portions. Pile each portion on individual serving dishes or plates into a small mound. Place the perilla leaves against each radish mound and rest 5 fish slices, like domino pieces, with a small dab of wasabi paste on the bottom corner. Serve with a small dish of tamari soy sauce on the side.

HOW TO CUT RECTANGULAR SLICES, HIRAZUKURI
Place the fillet lengthways, former skin-side up, 3cm (1¼in) away from the bottom of the chopping board, thicker side away from you. Assuming you are right-handed, keep the fillet in place with your left hand. Hold the knife so that the tip of the blade is slightly inclined to the left. Use the knife in a sweeping draw motion starting from the base to the tip, cutting gently through the fillet.

Start cutting at the right of the fillet. A 1cm (½in) slice is standard thickness. Firm-fleshed fish, such as sea bream or sea bass, may be cut into 5mm (¼in) slices and soft-fleshed fish, such as tuna, sardines or mackerel, into 1.5cm (⅝in) slices.

Wipe the knife clean occasionally with a clean, moist towel. Because of the way the knife is held, each slice will come to rest on the blade near the tip. Slide the knife, with the slice still attached, several centimetres away to the right, and then lay the slice on its right side. Repeat this process until the fillet is finished and you should have a neat row of "domino" slices on the right.

PAPER-THIN SASHIMI OF PLAICE
[HIRAME NO USU-ZUKURI]

Usu-zukuri, paper-thin slices, is most suitable for firm, white-fleshed fish, such as sea bream, sea bass or flounder. Think of this as the Japanese equivalent of Italy's carpaccio or Peruvian ceviche.

Serves 4

✳	✳	✳	✳	✳
250g (9oz) boneless and skinless plaice fillet	100g (3½oz) daikon (giant white radish), peeled	2 dried red chillies, deseeded	a few sprigs of chives, chopped	100ml (3½fl oz) Citrus Soy Vinegar (*see* page 158)

Wrap the fish in clingfilm and place it in the freezer. At the same time, chill four serving plates.

Meanwhile, make 2 holes in the radish with a chopstick, then plug the deseeded chillies into them using the chopstick. Grate the radish – the result will be rather watery, so lightly drain by either squeezing in your hand or wring in a clean piece of muslin or a tea towel.

Remove the fish from the freezer and unwrap. At the same time, take the serving plates out of the refrigerator.

Thinly slice the fish (*see* below) and immediately transfer each slice on to a plate (allow 5–7 slices each). Scatter the chopped chives on the top of the fish slices and make a small mound of grated chilli radish in the centre. Serve with a dish of citrus soy vinegar on the side.

PAPER-THIN SLICES, USU-ZUKURI
Wrap the fish in clingfilm and freeze for 10–15 minutes. You want the flesh to be firm enough to make thin slicing easier but not for it to become frozen.

Put a fillet on a chopping board, former skin-side up and thicker side away from you. Place your left hand on the left end of the fillet with enough pressure to hold it in place. Hold the knife so that the tip is tilted to the right and the blade is almost horizontal. Start at the left, positioning the base of the knife about 5mm (¼in) right of where your fingers are placed. Draw the blade from one o'clock to seven o'clock in a smooth controlled movement. You should have a thin slice resting at the tip of the knife.

Carefully transfer each slice immediately to a plate, overlapping the slices slightly to make a rosette. Add garnishes such as a curl of carrot, a scattering of finely chopped spring onion, or finely grated lemon zest.

HAND-ROLLED SUSHI [TEMAKI-ZUSHI]

Hand-rolls are quick and easy to make and do not require any specialist equipment.

Makes 8 hand-rolls

✳	✳	✳	✳	✳
4 sheets of nori, halved	400g (14oz) prepared sushi rice (see page 160)	4 teaspoons wasabi paste	200g (7oz) fish of your choice, cut into 6–7cm (2½–2¾in) long, pencil-sized strips	200g (7oz) vegetables such as cucumber, avocado, blanched carrot, fine green beans, cut into 6–7cm (2½–2¾in) long thin strips, rocket or mustard cress

Fold the sheets of nori in half across the grain and pinch along the folded edge, then pull them apart in halves – you should have four rectangular half nori sheets.

Hold a piece of halved rectangular nori in your left hand. Put a generous tablespoonful of rice on the top left corner of the nori and flatten it slightly. Dab a small amount of wasabi paste on the rice. Arrange your choice of fillings on top of the rice so that they point diagonally to the top left corner of the nori. Then bring the bottom left-hand corner of the nori towards the top side centre, wrapping it around the rice and fillings, forming a cornet. Repeat to make eight rolls in total.

THIN-ROLL SUSHI [H O S O - M A K I]

A thin roll has just a single filling, such as tuna, salmon or cucumber, cut into long thin strips, and uses a half nori sheet. Each roll is cut into six bite-sized pieces. The key to successful sushi-making is to have a clean, organized worktop. So, before you start, have all the ingredients and equipment ready.

Makes 4 rolls (24 pieces)

❁	❁	❁	❁	❁
2 sheets of nori	280–320g (10–11½oz) prepared sushi rice (see page 160)	2 teaspoons wasabi paste	150g (5½oz) tuna, cut into pencil-sized strips	sushi pickled ginger, to serve

Then put a half nori sheet horizontally shiny-side down on a bamboo rolling mat. Wet your hands with the vinegar water and take a handful of the rice weighing about 70–80g (2½–2¾oz) and roughly shape it into a log. Place the rice in the centre of the nori, then use your fingertips to spread it evenly over the nori leaving a 1–1.5cm (½–⅝in) border along the edge furthest from you. With your fingertips, press and make a groove along the centre of the rice and smear about ½ teaspoon of wasabi paste along it. Place a tuna strip in the wasabi groove.

To roll, lift up the edge of the mat closest to you with your thumbs and index fingers while keeping the filling in place with your middle and third fingers, and roll the mat over the tuna filling so that the top edge of the nori meets the edge of the rice. You should be able to see the uncovered nori strip. Lift the edge of the mat slightly and push the roll away from you so that the uncovered strip of nori seals the roll. Gently but firmly press the mat along the length of the roll using both hands to evenly shape it. Push in any stray grains of rice to tidy the ends. Set it aside in a cool place (but not in the refrigerator) while you make the remaining rolls in the same way.

Moisten a sharp kitchen knife with vinegar water, to prevent it from sticking. Cut each roll in the middle. Put the two halves next to each other and cut them twice to make six equal bite-sized pieces.

To serve, transfer on to a large platter or individual serving plates and serve with sushi pickled ginger and dark soy sauce on the side for dipping.

PRESSED SUSHI OF SMOKED SALMON

An *oshi-bako*, a press mould, is a specialist piece of equipment, available online, but you may not want to invest in one unless you are going to make sushi regularly. Alternatively, use an ordinary pastry cutter or a cooking ring.

Serves 4

✳	✳	✳	✳	✳
400g (14oz) prepared sushi rice (*see* page 160)	200g (7oz) smoked salmon	2 teaspoons wasabi paste	4 teaspoons salmon roe	2 teaspoons sake

Divide the rice into four equal portions. Using a cooking ring or a pastry cutter (about 8cm/3¼in diameter), stamp out four circles of smoked salmon. Do not worry about offcuts because they will be used to make edible garnishes later. Wet the cooking ring (to stop the rice from sticking) and place it in the centre of an individual plate.

Add a portion of sushi rice and press down firmly with the back of a dessertspoon so that the rice is compact and smooth over the top. Spread some wasabi paste evenly on top and gently lift up the ring. Place a smoked salmon circle on top. Repeat with the remaining rice portions and smoked salmon circles.

Cut the salmon offcuts into large rose petal shapes, then lay 3–5 pieces on the chopping board, overlapping, and roll up. Place a salmon rose on the top of each serving. Mix the salmon roe and sake together in a small bowl. Spoon a teaspoon of the roe mixture, slightly off-centre, over each rose and serve.

CHILLED SOBA WITH SPINACH AND WAKAME WITH SESAME DIPPING SAUCE

I came up with this idea when I was faced with a small mountain of home-grown spinach. The addition of spinach and wakame seaweed makes this dish very healthy and sesame dipping sauce gives it a satisfying depth.

Serves 2

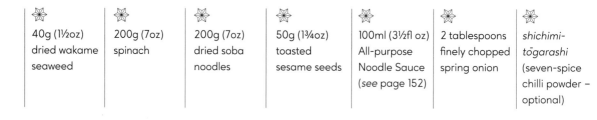

| 40g (1½oz) dried wakame seaweed | 200g (7oz) spinach | 200g (7oz) dried soba noodles | 50g (1¾oz) toasted sesame seeds | 100ml (3½fl oz) All-purpose Noodle Sauce (*see* page 152) | 2 tablespoons finely chopped spring onion | *shichimi-tōgarashi* (seven-spice chilli powder – optional) |

Put the seaweed in a bowl, cover with warm water, leave to soak for about 10 minutes, then drain. Cut the spinach into 10cm (4in) long pieces, removing any thick, tough stalks.

Cook the noodles as on page 154, but just before adding a cup of cold water, add the spinach and then the cold water, and let it return to the boil. Remove from the heat and drain, then plunge into cold water and rinse well. Drain thoroughly and divide between two baskets (or ordinary plates as long as the noodle mix is well drained).

To prepare the sesame dipping sauce, put the sesame seeds in a mortar and grind until it becomes a coarse paste. Gradually add the noodle sauce and adjust the taste by adding 2–3 tablespoons of water, then divide between two small cups.

Serve the noodles sprinkled with the finely chopped spring onion, *shichimi-tōgarashi*, if using, and the cups of dipping sauce on the side.

AVOCADO AND PRAWN ON SOBA WITH WASABI SAUCE

This is an adaptation of the rather retro dish, prawns in avocado.

Serves 2

200g (7oz) dried soba noodles	½ white or red onion	2–3 teaspoons wasabi paste	350ml 12fl oz) noodle pouring sauce (150ml/¼ pint All-purpose Noodle Sauce, see page 152, mixed with 100ml/3½fl oz water)	1 ripe avocado	10–12 cooked, peeled prawns	4 tablespoons cress

Cook the noodles as on page 164, drain and portion between two dishes.

Peel and finely slice the onion, then soak in a bowl of cold water for 10 minutes – this helps to remove the strong onion odour.

For the wasabi pouring sauce, combine the wasabi paste and the noodle pouring sauce, then divide between two small bowls.

Slice the avocado in half and remove the stone. Peel, then cut the flesh into bite-sized pieces. Drain the onion slices and place on top of the noodles. Arrange the avocado and prawns on top of the onion layer, then garnish with the cress. Serve with the wasabi pouring sauce on the side.

SAKE STEAMED CLAMS
[ASARI NO SAKE-MUSHI]

The advantage of steaming clams in sake is that the sake vaporizes at a lower temperature than water. This way, the sake works to cook the clams faster as well as erasing any fishy smell.

Serves 4

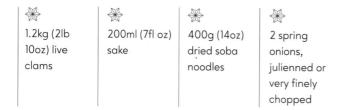

1.2kg (2lb 10oz) live clams	200ml (7fl oz) sake	400g (14oz) dried soba noodles	2 spring onions, julienned or very finely chopped

Combine 1 teaspoon of salt with 2 litres (3½ pints) of cold water in a large, flat-based container. Add the clams, cover tightly with foil and leave to stand for 2 hours at room temperature – this will help them spit out any grit and sand.

Wash the clams by gently rubbing them together under cold running water and drain. Discard any clams with damaged shells.

Put the clams in a large saucepan or frying pan with a tight-fitting lid over a medium heat. When hot, pour in 100ml (3½fl oz) of water, the sake and 2 teaspoons of light soy sauce and steam with the lid on for 3–5 minutes, until the cooking juices have been slightly reduced. Discard any clams that are not open.

Meanwhile, cook and drain the soba noodles (*see page 164*), then divide between four serving dishes. Spoon the clams over the noodles, scatter with the spring onions and serve.

JAPANESE-STYLE DUCK ORANGE

The famous French dish has been adapted with the addition of classic Japanese ingredients, yuzu, a type of citrus fruit, juice and refreshing daikon (giant white radish).

Serves 4

❈	❈	❈	❈	❈	❈
400g (14oz) daikon (giant white radish)	100g (3½oz) mizuna or rocket	4 tablespoons sake	2 tablespoons clear honey	2 tablespoons yuzu or lime or satsuma juice	4 x 140–160g (5–5¾oz) duck breasts, skin on

Peel the radish and cut it in half lengthways, then slice very thinly into half moons with a Japanese mandoline (or use a very steady hand and a sharp knife). Soak in cold water for 10 minutes, then drain. Put the radish, along with the mizuna or rocket, in the refrigerator to chill.

For the citrus dressing, put the sake in a small saucepan over a high heat to burn off the alcohol, then mix in the honey and yuzu, lime or satsuma juice along with 2 tablespoons of light soy sauce and set aside to cool.

Trim off any excess fat from the duck breasts, then with a very sharp knife, lightly score through the skin taking care not to cut into the flesh. Rub 4 teaspoons of salt into the skin.

Heat a large, heavy-based frying pan over a medium heat and brush with a scant amount of vegetable oil. Place the duck in the pan, skin-side down, and cook for 6–8 minutes to render the fat while spooning the fat over the flesh. Then turn over to cook the other side for 3–5 minutes.

Remove the duck from the pan, then pour boiling water over to wash off the fat and pat dry. Put the duck on a wire rack, skin-side up, and cover loosely with a piece of foil. Leave to rest for about 5 minutes. Do not wrap the duck tightly otherwise the crispy skin will go limp.

Take the radish and mizuna or rocket from the refrigerator and divide between four individual serving plates.

Place the duck, skin-side down, on a chopping board and cut each breast into 4–6mm (¼in) thick slices. Arrange the slices on the top of the vegetables, drizzle the citrus dressing over and serve.

OMELETTE PURSE SUSHI
[C H A K I N - Z U S H I | F U K U S A - Z U S H I]

Thin omelette makes a colourful edible wrapping material. *Chakin* is a small linen hand towel and *fukusa* is a large silk handkerchief, both are used in the traditional tea ceremony. However, in the context of sushi, *chakin-zushi* uses a round omelette, which is gathered and tied on the top, while for *fukusa-zushi*, a square sheet of omelette is used.

FOR CHAKIN-ZUSHI
Makes 8 purses

✳	✳	✳
400g (14oz) prepared sushi rice (*see* page 160)	8 thin omelettes (*see* page 163)	8 long sprigs of flat-leaf parsley or coriander

Place about 2 tablespoonfuls of sushi rice in the middle of a round omelette. Bring up the edges, gathering them on the top and tie with a sprig of flat-leaf parsley or coriander. Repeat with the remaining omelettes.

FOR FUKUSA-ZUSHI
Makes 8 purses

✳	✳	✳
400g (14oz) prepared sushi rice (*see* page 160)	8 thin omelettes (*see* page 163), round edges cut off each to make a square	8 long sprigs of flat-leaf parsley or coriander

Position 2 tablespoonfuls of sushi rice slightly off-centre on an omelette square. Bring up the lower corner over the filling, then fold in the side corners to meet at the centre, making a neat rectangular parcel. Tie the parcel with a sprig of flat-leaf parsley or coriander. Repeat with the remaining omelette squares.

SALT-GRILLED HORSE MACKEREL
[AJI NO SHIO-YAKI]

The Japanese like to see a whole fish on a plate. This is because fish, especially small ones, cook better on the bone.

Serves 4

✳	✳	✳
4 x 250–300g (9–10½oz) whole horse mackerel	200g (7oz) daikon (giant white radish), grated, to serve	4 lemon wedges, to serve

In a large bowl, mix 2 litres (3½ pints) of cold water with 50g (1¾oz) of salt – this is for washing the fish.

Start by removing the fish's prickly thorn-like scales along its sides, then remove the rest of the scales and gut – you may ask your fishmonger to do this. Wash off any traces of blood in the salt water, then pat dry with kitchen paper.

Make 2–3 shallow diagonal incisions on both sides. Sprinkle a teaspoonful of sea salt evenly all over each fish, use another teaspoonful to coat the fins for cosmetic effects, then set aside for about 10 minutes.

Meanwhile preheat the grill to the highest setting. Lightly oil the grill rack and return to the grill to heat.

Place the fish on the rack with the heads facing left and grill for 8–10 minutes. Carefully turn the fish over and continue grilling for a further 4–5 minutes.

Serve the fish with the head facing left on individual plates with a small mound of grated radish and a lemon wedge on the bottom right-hand corner of the plate.

COOK'S TIP
Try this with other small fish such as sardines, small sea bream or red mullet.

INSIDE-OUT-ROLL SUSHI [URA-MAKI]

Ura-maki are also sometimes known as Californian rolls. They were first created by an American-born Japanese chef in the early 1970s to accommodate squeamish American diners who were unsure about raw fish.

Ura-maki are deceptively easier to make than the traditional nori rolls. They are also more suited to advance preparations because the crispness of the nori is not the key element, as in the case of thin and thick rolls.

Makes 4 rolls (24 pieces)

✳	✳	✳	✳	✳	✳	✳
2 sheets of nori, halved	400–480g (14oz–1lb 1oz) prepared sushi rice (see page 160)	4 tablespoons ready-made mayonnaise	2 teaspoons wasabi paste	150g (5½oz) tuna, cut into 4 pencil-sized strips	20g (¾oz) fine green beans, trimmed and lightly steamed	½ prepared Dashi-rolled Omelette (see page 36), cut into 4 x 20cm (8in) long strips

Start by lining your bamboo rolling mat with clingfilm so that the rice will not stick on the mat.

Fold the sheets of nori in half across the grain and pinch along the folded edge, then pull them apart in halves – you should have four rectangular half nori sheets. Place a half sheet of nori on the mat. Dip your hands in a bowl of mild vinegar water to keep the rice from sticking, then take a large handful of the rice, weighing about 100–120g (3½–4¼oz), and place it in the middle of the nori. Wet your fingers again and spread the rice evenly to cover the entire surface of nori and pat it down slightly. Pick up the rice-covered nori and turn it over on the mat.

Mix the mayonnaise and wasabi paste together in a small bowl.

Lay one strip of tuna, a line of green beans and a strip of omelette along the centre of the nori on top of the wasabi. (Don't worry if some fillings stick out of the edges as it looks attractive when served.) To roll, lift up the nearest edge of the mat to you with your thumbs and index fingers, while holding the fillings in place with the rest of your fingers. Then start rolling to join the two edges rice-nori together. Lift up the front edge of the mat and push the roll away from you. Re-cover the roll with the mat and gently squeeze to shape into a round or square shape. ⟶

If you would like to coat the rolls in seasame seeds, spread out 1 tablespoon of toasted white or black sesame seeds on a large flat plate as evenly as possible, then roll the sushi roll in the seeds to coat all over. Set aside while you make the remaining rolls in the same way.

To cut, place a sushi roll on a chopping board, moisten a sharp kitchen knife with the vinegar water and cut the roll in half. Place the two halves next to each other, clean and moisten the knife, and cut them twice to give six equal bite-sized pieces.

To serve, transfer the cut pieces on to a platter or individual plates, arrange the pieces showing the cut-side up. Serve with a mound of sushi pickled ginger and some soy sauce, if desired.

ALTERNATIVE FLAVOURINGS
White crabmeat with avocado and cucumber strips
Salmon with cucumber strips and finely chopped spring onion
Cooked prawns with mustard cress and omelette strips

FAST

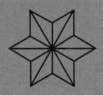

DASHI-ROLLED OMELETTE
[DASHI-MAKI] TAMAGO

This soft, succulent, dashi-infused omelette makes a delicious and healthy meal. It is helpful if you have a Japanese omelette pan, but a regular round pan can be used – simply cut off the round edges after cooking.

Makes 4 rolls

❋	❋	❋
1 tablespoon mirin	12 eggs	about 200g (7oz) daikon (giant white radish), grated and lightly drained

In a large bowl, mix together 480ml (17fl oz) of Primary or Vegetarian Dashi (*see* pages 143 and 147), the mirin, 2 tablespoons of light soy sauce and ½ teaspoon of salt until the salt dissolves. In a separate bowl, lightly beat the eggs and then add them to the dashi mixture. Roughly combine and divide into four portions.

Place the omelette pan over a medium heat and lightly oil the pan with vegetable oil using folded kitchen paper. Heat the pan, then drop in a spoonful of the egg mixture – if it sizzles a little, the pan is ready.

Ladle about one-third of one portion of egg mixture into the pan and quickly spread to thinly cover the surface. Cook over a medium heat until the surface begins to set, then fold towards you in quarter sections using either chopsticks or a spatula. Push the folded omelette to the far end of the pan and re-oil the exposed surface of the pan. Ladle in another third of the egg mixture and gently lift the folded omelette to allow the egg mixture to get under it to cover the entire pan. When the egg begins to set, fold it towards you in quarters with the first roll at the centre. If you are using a square pan, shape the omelette by gently pressing it against the side of the pan. Repeat the process – re-oil, add the last third of the portion of egg mixture, cook and fold.

Remove the omelette on to a bamboo rolling mat placed on a chopping board. Wrap the omelette with the rolling mat and shape while it is warm – traditionally a rectangular brick, but you can also make a round, cylinder. Keep the omelette wrapped in the rolling mat while you make three more rolls.

Mix the grated radish with 2 tablespoons of dark soy sauce. Cut each omelette into about 1.5cm (⅝in) thick slices and arrange on individual serving plates. Put about a tablespoonful of mound of radish/soy on the side and serve at room temperature.

JAPANESE IN 7

TUNA CUBES WITH WASABI AVOCADO DRESSING

Cube-cut is most probably the easiest sashimi cut of all, especially in the West where tuna is often sold in a steak form.

Serves 4

✳	✳	✳	✳
1 very ripe avocado	2 tablespoons rice vinegar	1 tablespoon wasabi powder mixed with 1 tablespoon water to form a paste	2 x 200g (7oz) tuna steaks cut into 2cm (¾in) cubes (see Tip)

Cut the avocado in half and remove the stone. Peel, then roughly chop the flesh. Use a fork to mash the avocado into a smooth paste in a large bowl. Add the rice vinegar, wasabi paste and 1 tablespoon of dark soy sauce and mix well.

Add the tuna cubes and combine, ensuring each cube is coated with the avocado mixture. Serve immediately.

COOK'S TIP
This style of cutting, *kaku-zukuri,* is suitable for fish with thick but tender-fleshed fillets such as tuna, salmon and bonito. Choose 2cm (¾in) thick steaks and cut them into 2cm (¾in) wide strips, but do not separate the strips. Rotate the strips 90° and cut straight down at 2cm (¾in) intervals to form cubes.

CLAM AND SAMPHIRE [MISO SOUP ASARI]

This recipe is more suited to adventurous cooks who go foraging on wild shores. For me, it brings back fond childhood memories of shellfish gathering, which was a fun and highly rewarding activity in spring just as the sea was beginning to warm up. Nowadays, gladly or regrettably, depending on your point of view, it is possible to buy both clams and samphire from fishmongers without venturing on to a shore.

Serves 4

| 400g (14oz) live clams (*see* Tip) | 80g (2¾oz) samphire, trimmed | 40g (1½oz) white miso | 30g (1oz) red miso |

Wash and clean the clams by gently rubbing the shells together. Put the clams in a saucepan with 800ml (28fl oz) of water and bring to the boil over a gentle heat while constantly skimming away any scum that floats to the surface. When the shells begin to open, add the samphire, increase the heat to let the soup return to the boil and cook for 1–2 minutes. Discard any unopened clams.

The soup must be served hot, so warm four soup bowls with hot (not boiling) water.

Put the miso pastes into a small bowl and add a ladleful of the soup broth to soften, stir well. Pour the mixture into the soup and bring back to the boil for a second. Turn off the heat and serve immediately in the warmed bowls.

COOK'S TIP

Shopping and careful selection of ingredients is an important part of good cooking. Choose clams with perfect shells. You can tell whether a clam is alive or not by tapping two together – if it sounds metallic, the clams are most likely still fresh and they will open up when heated. But if the sound is dull, they are dead and should be discarded before cooking. Before cooking, cover the clams with lightly salted water for a few hours in a cool, dark place – this will help them spit out any sand or dirt.

CHILLED SOBA IN BASKET [ZARU SOBA]

The Japanese summer is relentlessly hot and punishingly humid, and many people lose their appetite except for these chilled noodles. *Zaru soba* literally means "noodles in basket" and they are served on basketwork or bamboo boxes with slatted bottoms, accompanied by cold dipping sauce. It is a simple and refreshing summer favourite.

Serves 2

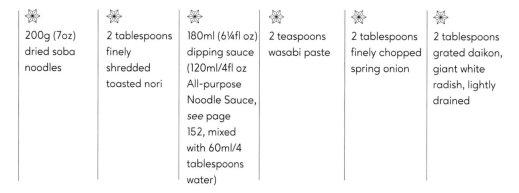

| 200g (7oz) dried soba noodles | 2 tablespoons finely shredded toasted nori | 180ml (6¼fl oz) dipping sauce (120ml/4fl oz All-purpose Noodle Sauce, *see* page 152, mixed with 60ml/4 tablespoons water) | 2 teaspoons wasabi paste | 2 tablespoons finely chopped spring onion | 2 tablespoons grated daikon, giant white radish, lightly drained |

Cook the noodles as on page 164, but do not reheat. Divide them between two baskets (or ordinary plates, as long as the noodles are well drained).

To serve, sprinkle the shredded nori over each serving of noodles. Serve the dipping sauce in individual cups or small bowls alongside. Place the wasabi paste, spring onion and daikon in small dishes and let each diner help themselves.

To eat, mix a dab of wasabi and some spring onion with grated radish in the dipping sauce. Pick up some noodles and dip into the sauce mixture.

BEEF UDON [NIKU UDON]

Beef gives extra meaty depth to otherwise simple, plain-tasting noodle dishes. Japanese beef is butchered differently from Western beef and, in general, meat is sold thinly sliced.

Serves 2

✻	✻	✻	✻	✻
160g (5¾oz) minute steak or silverside	1 young leek, white part only	300ml (½ pint) All-purpose Noodle Sauce (*see* page 152)	200g (7oz) dried udon noodles	*sansho*, Japanese pepper, to taste

Slice the beef into thin 4–5cm (½–2in) long pieces. Cut the leek into 1cm (½in) thick slices on the diagonal.

Heat 2 teaspoons of vegetable oil in a saucepan over a medium heat and just before adding the beef, place the bottom of the pan on a cool, damp cloth (this stops the meat sticking to the base), then add the beef and cook for 1 minute. Pour in 400ml (14fl oz) of water and bring to the boil, skimming off any scum that floats to the surface. Add the leek and noodle sauce and reduce the heat to a gentle simmer while you cook the noodles.

Cook the noodles as on page 164, drain and portion between two warmed bowls. Ladle in the soup broth and sprinkle over *sansho* pepper to taste. Serve immediately.

PAN-FRIED ASPARAGUS WITH SOY AND SESAME

Asparagus, although a relative newcomer to Japanese cuisine, is loved for its taste and prized for its tantalizingly short season.

Serves 4

12–16 asparagus spears	2 tablespoons sake	1 teaspoon toasted white sesame seeds, to serve

Asparagus has a natural breaking point below which it is stringy and inedible – hold a spear between your hands then bend until it breaks, and discard the lower part. Cut each trimmed spear on the diagonal into 4cm (1½in) length pieces.

Heat 1 tablespoon of sesame oil in a frying pan over a medium heat. Add the thicker pieces of asparagus first, followed by the rest, shaking the pan to toss, and cook for 2–3 minutes. Add the sake and 2 teaspoons of dark soy sauce and continue to cook while still shaking the pan until most of the liquid has evaporated.

Portion on to four plates, then sprinkle the sesame seeds over and serve.

PAN-FRIED SCALLOPS WITH BROCCOLI
[HOTATE TO BUROKKORT NO ITAME-MONO]

Itame-mono is difficult to translate – pan-frying, shallow-frying, sautéing, or even stir-frying – the method is never listed separately in Japanese cookbooks. This is because in reality, *itame-mono* dishes are more like a Japanese version of Chinese stir-fry. It is arguably the easiest and quickest cooking method of all.

Serves 4

✺	✺	✺	✺	✺	✺
400g (14oz) shelled scallops, without roe	400g (14oz) sprouting broccoli, trimmed	2 eggs, lightly beaten	2 tablespoons plain flour	4 tablespoons sake	freshly ground black pepper

Slice the scallops in half horizontally and sprinkle ½ teaspoon of salt over, then leave to stand for 10–15 minutes.

Meanwhile, heat 1 tablespoon of vegetable oil in a large frying pan or wok over a high heat, add the broccoli and toss, then add 400ml (14fl oz) of water. Bring to the boil for 1–2 minutes, then drain and keep the broccoli warm.

Wipe the pan clean with kitchen paper. Heat another tablespoon of vegetable oil over a medium heat and add the eggs. Use two pairs of chopsticks to stir constantly for 3–5 minutes to make scrambled eggs. Remove and keep warm.

Spread the scallops over kitchen paper and pat dry. Dust with the flour. Heat another tablespoon of vegetable oil in the same pan over a high heat and quickly sear the scallops on both sides. Add the broccoli and scrambled eggs to the scallops and toss to mix. Pour in the sake and 2 tablespoons of light soy sauce, stir and bring to the boil for a minute, then adjust the seasoning with salt and pepper. Divide between four dishes and serve.

VARIATION
Try this recipe with shelled raw tiger prawns in place of the scallops.

HIJIKI IN TOFU DRESSING
[HIJIKI NO SHIRO AE]

This is a quick and easy recipe that is light in texture and full of high-quality protein from the tofu and rich in calcium, iron and magnesium from the hijiki.

Serves 4

8 tablespoons dried hijiki	1 medium carrot, peeled and julienned	1 abura-age (deep-fried tofu)	2 tablespoons toasted white sesame seeds	1 tablespoon white caster or granulated sugar	4 tablespoons Tofu Dressing (see page 148)

Put the hijiki in a bowl, pour over enough water to cover and leave to stand for 10–15 minutes. Drain through a sieve and press down on the *hijiki* with a rubber spatula, then leave to drain further while you prepare the other ingredients.

Parboil the carrot strips in salted water for 1 minute and drain. Set aside.

Put the deep-fried tofu in a sieve and pour boiling water on both sides to remove excess oil, then pat dry with kitchen paper. Slice in half lengthways and cut into thin strips.

Put the sesame seeds and sugar in a *suribachi*, a Japanese mortar, and grind until about half of the seeds are still visible. Transfer to a mixing bowl. Add 2 tablespoons of light soy sauce and the tofu dressing and mix well. Add the drained hijiki, carrot and deep-fried tofu strips and use a rubber spatula to lightly mix.

Divide between four individual dishes and serve.

SERVING SUGGESTION
To add a contemporary touch, I often serve this classic dish in Little Gem lettuce leaves or scooped-out tomatoes. Cucumber cups or celery sticks also make attractive edible serving vessels.

TUNA AND ROCKET ON SOBA

This tasty noodle salad couldn't be easier to make – the only cooking involved is preparing the noodles. The rest is just a simple assembly job. The all-purpose noodle sauce doubles up as a salad dressing and noodle sauce.

Serves 2

✻	✻	✻	✻	✻	✻	✻
200g (7oz) dried soba noodles	350ml (12fl oz) noodle pouring sauce (150ml/¼ pint All-purpose Noodle Sauce, *see* page 152, mixed with 100ml/3½fl oz water)	1 teaspoon grated fresh ginger	1 teaspoon toasted sesame seeds	100g (3½oz) rocket	240g (8¾oz) can tuna in spring water, drained	*shichimi-tōgarashi* (seven-spice chilli powder), to serve (optional)

Cook the noodles as on page 164, drain and portion between two dishes.

For the pouring sauce, put the noodle pouring sauce, ginger and toasted sesame seeds in a lidded glass jar, along with 2 teaspoons of dark soy sauce and 1 teaspoon of sesame oil, and shake well to mix.

Place the rocket on top of the soba, then place the drained tuna on top.

Pour the sauce over the noodle arrangement. Sprinkle with *shichimi-tōgarashi*, if using, and serve.

HOT SPRING EGGS ON ASPARAGUS
[ONSEN-TAMAGO TO ASUPARA]

There are countless hot springs in Japan and many people enjoy these natural resources, even for cooking. *Onsen-tamago*, hot spring eggs, as the name implies is where the eggs are cooked by sitting in warm water. This is a perfect healthy vegetarian dish.

Serves 4

| 4 very fresh eggs | 20 asparagus spears, trimmed | 2 teaspoons toasted white sesame seeds |

If the eggs are kept in the refrigerator, take them out 20–30 minutes before you begin cooking.

Pour 1 litre (1¾ pints) of water into a saucepan, bring to the boil and then remove from the heat. Add 200ml (7fl oz) of cold water and stir.

Put the eggs (still in their shells) in the pan, cover with a lid and leave for 12 minutes.

Meanwhile, steam the asparagus for 3–5 minutes and then sprinkle with ½ teaspoon of salt. Divide the asparagus between four plates, sprinkle each portion with 1 teaspoon of dark soy sauce and ½ teaspoon of sesame seeds, then loosely cover with cooking foil to keep warm.

Remove the eggs from the pan and wait for 3 minutes before cracking them open over the asparagus, then serve.

TUNA HOTPOT [NEGIMA-NABE]

The name of this hotpot is an abbreviation of *negi*, spring onion, and *maguro*, tuna. It is hard to believe but some 250 years ago when tuna was plentiful, the fatty belly of tuna was considered an inferior cut, while residents of Edo, old Tokyo, prized the lean back part for their favourite sushi. This dish was invented as a cheap food for ordinary people. I use leeks instead of the traditional spring onions because Japanese spring onions are much larger than their Western counterparts and taste more similar to leeks.

Serves 4

| 400g (14oz) tuna steak | 4 thin leeks, cleaned and trimmed | 100ml (3½fl oz) sake | 4 tablespoons white caster or granulated sugar | shichimi-tōgarashi (seven-spice chilli powder), to serve |

Cut the tuna into 1cm (½in) thick bite-sized slices. Cut the leeks into 3cm (1¼in) long pieces.

Put the leeks, sake, sugar, 100ml (3½fl oz) of dark soy sauce and 400ml (14fl oz) of water in a casserole pot and bring to the boil over a medium-low heat. When the broth begins to boil, add the tuna slices and cook for 3–5 minutes.

Divide between four individual serving bowls and serve with the *shichimi-tōgarashi* on the side.

VARIATION
You may also like to try this recipe with yellowtail.

ASPARAGUS AND SCRAMBLED EGG SCATTERED SUSHI

I like to serve this sushi in late spring when asparagus is in season and at its best.

Serves 4

500g (1lb 2oz) asparagus spears, trimmed	2 eggs, beaten	2 teaspoons white caster or granulated sugar	400g (14oz) prepared sushi rice (see page 160)	1 tablespoon toasted white sesame seeds	1 sheet of nori, crumbled

Steam the asparagus for 3–4 minutes, rinse under cold running water to refresh, then drain. Reserve the tips for the garnish and chop the spears into small pieces on the diagonal.

Mix the eggs with the sugar, 2 tablespoons of light soy sauce and ½ teaspoon of salt in a small mixing bowl. Heat 1–2 tablespoons of vegetable oil in a non-stick omelette pan over a medium heat. Pour the egg mixture into the pan and cook, stirring all the time with either an egg whisk or two pairs of chopsticks. When the egg begins to set, remove from the heat but continue to stir to get a fluffy consistency.

Mix the sushi rice with the chopped asparagus and half the scrambled eggs. Transfer to a large serving dish or divide between four individual bowls. Spread the remaining scrambled eggs over, sprinkle the sesame seeds on top and arrange the reserved asparagus tips in the centre. Scatter over the crumbled nori and serve.

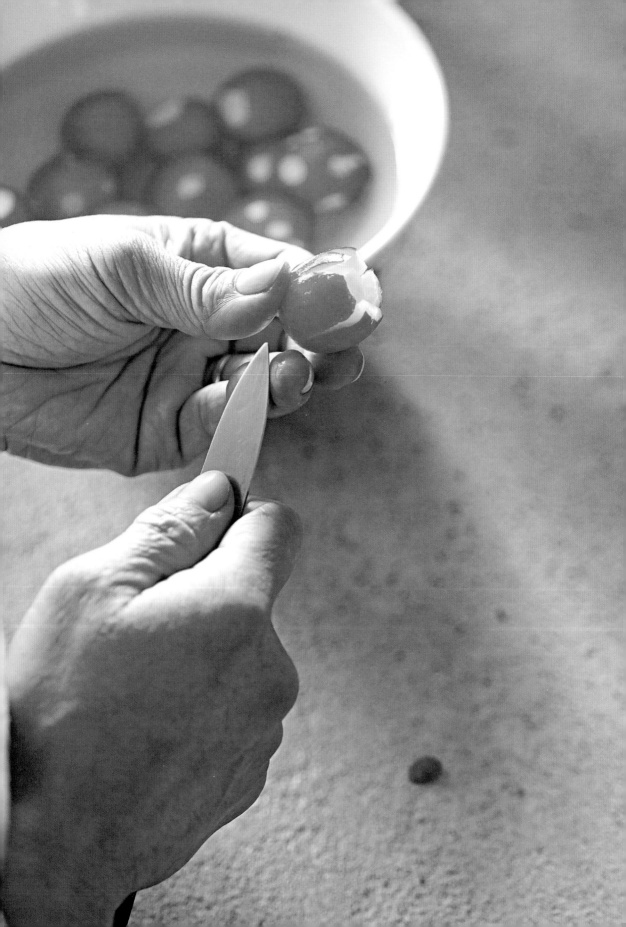

LIGHT

TIGER PRAWN CLEAR SOUP
[EBI NO SUIMONO]

This is another classic clear soup that is relatively easy to prepare at home. I have substituted *mitsuba*, trefoil Japanese wild chervil, with coriander leaves.

Serves 4

8 unshelled raw tiger prawns each weighing 20g (¾oz)	2 tablespoons cornflour, for dusting	1 tablespoon sake	4 sprigs of coriander	finely shredded zest of ½ lemon

Shell the prawns, remove the heads but leave the tails, and devein. Reserve the shells and heads. Wash the prawns and pat dry with kitchen paper, then lightly sprinkle with salt and dust with the cornflour. Bring a pan of 600ml (20fl oz) of water with 1 teaspoon of salt added to the boil and blanch the prawns for 2 minutes, then drain and keep warm.

Meanwhile, put the reserved shells and heads in a separate pan with 600ml (20fl oz) of Primary Dashi (*see* page 143) and bring to just below the boil over a medium heat. Reduce the heat to low and simmer for 3–5 minutes until the prawn shells turn bright red, then remove from the dashi using a slotted spoon and discard.

Season the dashi with the sake, 1 tablespoon of light soy sauce and some salt according to your taste.

The soup must be served hot, so warm four soup bowls with hot (not boiling) water.

Arrange two prawns, tails up, in each warmed bowl, place a sprig of coriander and a little finely grated lemon zest in between the prawns. Carefully ladle in the seasoned dashi around the prawns so that it does not splash and disturb the arrangement, and serve immediately.

SWIRLING EGG CLEAR SOUP
[KAKITAMA-JIRU]

This is probably one of the most popular clear soups that is made more often at home rather than in restaurants. It is easy to make, visually pleasing, nourishing and very tasty.

Serves 4

❋	❋	❋	❋	❋
1 tablespoon sake	2 tablespoons cornflour mixed with 2 tablespoons cold water	2 eggs, lightly beaten	½ teaspoon finely grated lemon zest	2 tablespoons cress, to garnish

The soup must be served hot, so warm four soup bowls with hot (not boiling) water.

In a saucepan, bring 600ml (20fl oz) of Primary Dashi (*see* page 143) to just below the boil, then simmer over a low heat. Season to taste with the sake, 1 tablespoon of light soy sauce and some salt. Add the cornflour mixture and stir for 30 seconds to thicken.

Slowly pour in the beaten eggs in a spiral over the entire surface of the soup. Resist the urge to stir immediately, but wait for about 30 seconds to allow the eggs to settle and then stir gently with a wire whisk for about a minute. The eggs should form thread-like filaments.

Finally, add the lemon zest and immediately remove from the heat. Ladle the soup into the warmed bowls, garnish with the cress and serve immediately.

RED MISO SOUP OF SEA BREAM
[TAI NO AKA-DASHI]

Aka-miso or *aka-dashi*, dark red miso, is generally reserved for soups. Red miso soup is considered rather sophisticated and is served in expensive restaurants.

Serves 4

✳	✳	✳	✳	✳	✳
200g (7oz) boneless sea bream fillet	1 postcard-sized piece of dried kelp	4 asparagus spears, cut into 3–4cm (1¼–1½in) pieces on the diagonal	40g (1½oz) red miso	pinch or so of cress, to garnish	*sansho* (Japanese pepper), to serve

Cut the sea bream into large bite-sized pieces, sprinkle with 1 teaspoon of salt and set aside on a plate lined with kitchen paper for 10–15 minutes. Pat dry with kitchen paper.

Put the kelp in a saucepan with 800ml (28fl oz) of Primary Dashi (*see* page 143) and slowly bring to just below the boil over a low heat. When small bubbles begin to appear, add the asparagus. Place the fish in a small sieve and blanch in the dashi for 3–4 minutes or until the fish is just cooked. Remove the fish and asparagus and keep warm. Let the dashi return to a gentle simmer, then remove the kelp and discard.

The soup must be served hot, so warm your soup bowls with hot (not boiling) water.

Put the miso in a small bowl with a ladleful of the dashi broth and mix well to soften, then pour into the soup. Let the soup reach just below the boil and then turn off the heat immediately.

Arrange the fish, skin-side up, and the asparagus in the warmed soup bowls and carefully ladle in the soup. Garnish with a little cress in the centre of each bowl, sprinkle the *sansho* pepper over and serve.

SAVOURY EGG TOFU [TAMAGO-DŌFU]

A deliciously light, savoury egg custard, that is usually served chilled. Although this dish is named "tofu", due to its soft, smooth texture, bean curd is not an ingredient in this dish. The one simple rule to follow if adjusting this recipe to serve any number, is to use equal amounts of dashi to the volume of beaten eggs. Start this dish the day before you intend to serve.

Serves 4

✳	✳	✳	✳
6 eggs (about 300ml/½ pint), well beaten	1½ tablespoons mirin	2 cherry tomatoes, halved	4 basil leaves

Line a 20cm (8in) square baking tin (a chocolate brownie tin is ideal because of its clean edges) with foil so that the foil extends over two opposite sides of the tin by 5cm (2in) at each end. Ensure the foil is not wrinkled at the bottom and do not oil or butter.

Pour the eggs through a sieve into a large bowl. In another bowl, mix together 300ml (½ pint) of Primary Dashi or Vegetarian Dashi (see pages 143 and 147), ½ tablespoon of salt, the mirin and 3 tablespoons of light soy sauce until the salt is dissolved completely. Stir the eggs into the dashi mixture until evenly mixed. Pour the mixture through a fine mesh sieve again back into the bowl, ensuring it is thoroughly combined.

Gently pour the egg mixture into the prepared tin and spoon off any tiny bubbles on the surface. Place the tin in a bain-marie, resting it on chopsticks or a folded towel so that the bottom of the tin is insulated from the base of the bain-marie. Insulate further by placing more folded towels around the sides of the tin. Cover the tin by gently placing a single sheet of crinkled foil over the top like a tent. All those protective measures are to ensure that the "tofu" is only cooked by an even, gentle heat to give a soft and smooth texture. Fill the bain-marie with hot water halfway up the sides of the tin.

Put the tin and bain-marie in a steamer and steam over a high heat for 3 minutes. Reduce the heat to low and continue steaming for a further 25 minutes. Or, if you don't have a large steamer, place the arrangement in a large baking tray filled with hot water up to just below the depth of the arrangement and place in a preheated oven at 220°C/425°F/gas mark 7 for 30 minutes. The "tofu" is done when a cocktail stick inserted into the centre comes out clean. Do not worry about any clear broth seeping out of the hole made by the cocktail stick – this will reseal. The custard should not be dry nor firm but wobble a little if you tap the side. Carefully lift the tin out of the steamer or the oven and allow it to cool a little before refrigerating overnight.

Lift out the custard by picking up the two ends of the foil and transferring it to a chopping board, still resting on the foil. Cut into four blocks. Place each block in a dish. Garnish with half a cherry tomato and a basil leaf on the centre of each block and serve.

SOY-BUTTERED CORN

This simple dish makes a tasty accompaniment to barbecued meats.

Serves 4

2 corn on the cob, halved	30g (1oz) butter, melted	1 teaspoon caster sugar

Preheat the grill to high. Line a grill pan with foil.

Put the corn in a large saucepan and cover with lightly salted water. Bring to the boil over a high heat and cook for 5–7 minutes. Drain and put the corn on the metal rack of the lined grill pan.

Mix the melted butter, sugar and 4 teaspoons of dark soy sauce together and brush generously over the corn. Place under the grill to cook for 5–8 minutes, while turning and basting regularly, until slightly blistered.

Brush any remaining butter mixture over the corn and serve immediately.

SPINACH AND TOFU JELLY

This is a very pretty, delicious and healthy starter that you can prepare in advance. *Kanten* (agar-agar) is the Japanese equivalent of gelatine but is made from a seaweed called Ceylon moss and hence is vegetarian. It is also ten times more coagulant and completely fat- and virtually calorie-free. Because it is rich in calcium, iron and edible fibre this makes it an ideal diet food.

Serves 4

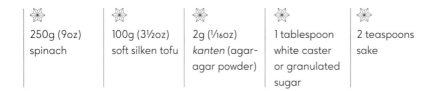

250g (9oz) spinach	100g (3½oz) soft silken tofu	2g (¹⁄₁₆oz) *kanten* (agar-agar powder)	1 tablespoon white caster or granulated sugar	2 teaspoons sake

Cook the spinach in salted boiling water for 30 seconds and drain very well. With a food mixer or food processor, blitz the cooked spinach into a thick paste. Roughly break up the tofu with your hands.

Put 250ml (9fl oz) of Vegetarian Dashi (*see* page 147) and the *kanten* in a saucepan and dissolve over a medium heat, stirring. Bring to the boil for 2 minutes. Add the tofu, sugar, sake and ½ teaspoon of salt. When the tofu begins to float to the surface, turn off the heat.

Add the spinach paste and stir once or twice to mix through, then pour the mixture into a mould (15 x 20 x 4cm/6 x 8 x 1½in) and leave to set at room temperature, before transferring to the refrigerator to chill until ready to serve. (*Kanten* sets at 40°C/104°F, which is higher than normal room temperature.) Turn out of the mould, cut into thick slices and serve with a drizzle of tamari.

A NOTE ON TAMARI

Tamari is a type of soy sauce, but unlike dark or light soy sauce, it is made from pure soya beans with no addition of wheat. It is dark, thick and slightly sweet in taste and is used for dipping sashimi and sushi.

MUSHROOM IN SESAME MISO DRESSING
[KINOKO NO GOMA MISO AE]

I am delighted that some exotic oriental mushrooms have become so much easier to find in Western supermarkets.

Serves 4

4–6 shiitake mushrooms, stems discarded	50g (1¾oz) shimeji mushrooms	50g (1¾oz) enoki mushrooms	2 tablespoons toasted white sesame seeds, plus 2 teaspoons, to garnish	1 tablespoon white caster or granulated sugar	4 tablespoons white or light-coloured miso

Cut the caps of the shiitake mushrooms into thin slices. Both shimeji and enoki mushrooms are joined at the base, so cut off and discard the bases and separate the stems with your hands.

In a saucepan, bring 500ml (18fl oz) of water to the boil, add 120ml (4fl oz) of dark soy sauce and all the mushrooms, then parboil for 1 minute. Drain thoroughly and leave to stand in a sieve to continue draining.

Put the 2 tablespoons of toasted sesame seeds and the sugar in a *suribachi*, a Japanese mortar, and grind until most of the seeds are crushed.

Add the miso and 2 tablespoons of dark soy sauce and mix. You may need to add more soy sauce to soften the mixture to the consistency of double cream.

Press down on the mushrooms with your hand to drain any excess liquid, then add to the dressing and mix in the *suribachi*.

Divide the mushroom mixture into four equal portions to serve in neat mounds in individual serving dishes, sprinkle with the remaining toasted sesame seeds and serve.

JAPANESE ONION SOUP
[TAMANEGI NO MOSI-SHIRU]

This is the Japanese answer to the famous French onion soup. The slow-cooked onions give a sweet flavour to the broth.

Serves 4

✳	✳	✳	✳
800g (1lb 12oz) onions, thinly sliced	800ml (28fl oz) soft mineral water	40g (1½oz) medium-coloured miso	2 teaspoons finely chopped flat-leaf parsley, to serve

Put about 40g (1½oz) of the onion slices in a bowl of cold water and set aside. Put the rest of the onions in a heavy-based saucepan with 2 tablespoons of vegetable oil. Place a piece of dampened greaseproof paper directly on top of the onions. Cover tightly with a lid and cook over a very low heat, stirring occasionally, until the onions are tender – this will take 30–40 minutes.

Remove the paper, add the mineral water to the pan and bring to the boil over a high heat. Put the miso in a small bowl, add a ladleful of soup broth and mix to soften the mixture, then return to the soup. Taste and adjust the seasoning with light soy sauce, if necessary, and let the soup return to the boil. Once at the boil, turn off the heat immediately.

The soup must be served hot, so warm four soup bowls with hot (not boiling) water.

Drain the soaked onion slices. Divide the soup between the warmed soup bowls, add the drained onion slices, garnish with the parsley and serve.

VINEGAR SQUEEZED SPRING CABBAGE
[KYABETSU NO SUMOMIAE]

This dish combines two traditional techniques – *momi*, squeezing, and *su-ae*, vinegar-dressed.

Serves 4

❋	❋	❋	❋
500g (1lb 2oz) spring cabbage	1 carrot, peeled	30g (1oz) fresh ginger, peeled	6 tablespoons Sweet Vinegar (*see* page 158)

Cut the cabbage into 2–3cm (¾–1¼in) squares and discard the thick cores. Cut the carrot and ginger into 3cm (1¼in) long matchsticks.

Put the cabbage, carrot and ginger in a large, ziplock plastic bag and sprinkle over 2 teaspoons of salt, then seal and with your hands squeeze the bag for 2–3 minutes as if you are massaging it. A great deal of liquid will come out as the cabbage begins to wilt. Drain off the liquid.

Add 4 tablespoons of the sweet vinegar to the bag, reseal, then squeeze again for a further 2–3 minutes. Drain off as much liquid as possible.

Divide the cabbage mixture between four individual serving bowls and drizzle ½ tablespoon of the remaining sweet vinegar over each portion, then serve.

GREEN BEANS AND CARROT IN WHITE SESAME DRESSING
[INGEN TO NINJIN NO SHIRO-GOMA AE]

Sesame dressing is a quick and easy way to transform otherwise rather ordinary vegetables.

Serves 4

100g (3½oz) fine green beans	1 medium carrot, peeled	4 tablespoons White Sesame Dressing (see page 150)

Trim the beans and cut into half lengths. Thinly slice the carrot into 3cm (1¼in) long julienne strips. Parboil the vegetables separately in lightly salted boiling water for 2 minutes each, then rinse in cold water and drain thoroughly. Pat them dry with kitchen paper.

Put the vegetables in a bowl, then add 2 tablespoons of light soy sauce. Use your hands to mix and lightly squeeze them – this adds a subtle soy flavour to the vegetables.

Transfer the vegetable mixture to another bowl, add the white sesame dressing and toss. Divide the mixture into four equal portions and serve in neat mounds in individual dishes.

RED RICE [OKOWA / SEKIHAN]

You will need a bamboo steamer for this recipe and to start the day before you intend serving it.

Serves 4

❋	❋	❋
80g (2¾oz) dried adzuki beans	400g (14oz) *mochigome* (glutinous rice)	1 teaspoon toasted black sesame seeds

Soak the beans in cold water for 3–4 hours, then drain. Parboil for 5 minutes in fresh water, then drain, change the water and repeat the process.

Put the beans in a saucepan with 400ml (14fl oz) of water, bring to the boil, uncovered, then simmer for 10 minutes or until the water turns reddish. Drain the beans, reserving the water. Using a ladle held high above another bowl, aerate and cool the water 5–6 times to brighten the colour.

Wash and rinse the rice (*see* page 167), put in a pan with the reserved red water and leave to stand overnight or up to 24 hours; this tints the rice pink. Drain and reserve 200ml (7fl oz) of the water. Add 1 teaspoon of salt to the water and set aside.

Fill a saucepan with plenty of water and bring to a rapid boil. Mix the rice and beans evenly and spread out on a damp cloth in a bamboo steamer. Place this over the saucepan, steam over a high heat for 20 minutes, then lift off the lid and sprinkle over a tablespoon of the reserved red salted water. Repeat this several times, continuing to steam over a high heat for a further 15–20 minutes.

Mix the toasted sesame seeds with ½ teaspoon of sea salt in a small bowl. If you are not serving straight away, the rice needs to be cooled down quickly and chilled, and can then be served cold. Serve in individual bowls, sprinkled with the sesame salt.

COOK'S TIP
Compared to normal short-grain rice, glutinous rice contains more starch (amylopectin) that gives it its characteristics stickiness. In Japan it is used to make red rice with adzuki beans or pounded to make mochi/rice cake.

VINEGARED CUCUMBER
[KYŪRI NO SUNOMONO]

Here is a quick and easy and, above all, very healthy dish – it can be served as a vegetarian starter or as a side for meaty dishes.

Serves 4

✿	✿	✿	✿	✿
2 tablespoons dried wakame	4 Lebanese cucumbers or 2 standard cucumbers	thumb-sized piece of fresh ginger, peeled and thinly sliced	120ml (4fl oz) Three-flavour Vinegar (see page 156)	2 teaspoons toasted white sesame seeds, to garnish

Put four individual serving dishes in the refrigerator to chill.

Soften the dried wakame by covering it with plenty of warm water in a bowl for 10 minutes. Drain.

Thinly slice the cucumbers (if using standard cucumbers, peel and cut in half lengthways and scoop out the central seeds). Put the cucumber slices and the ginger in a medium-sized, non-metallic mixing bowl, sprinkle with the 1 tablespoon of salt, then squeeze with your hands for about 1 minute. A fair amount of water will come out, and the aim is to squeeze and drain off as much liquid as possible.

Add the wakame and 1 tablespoon of the vinegar to the cucumber, then lightly mix. Squeeze and drain away any excess liquid. Add a further 4 tablespoons of the vinegar, mix and drain again. Finally, pour in the remaining vinegar and mix lightly. The reason for staging the vinegar addition is to avoid the finished dish becoming watery.

Divide into four equal portions, gently squeeze and drain any excess liquid before arranging in small mounds in the chilled dishes. Sprinkle over the sesame seeds to garnish and serve.

VEGAN

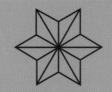

SOY-STEEPED MUSHROOMS

I am delighted to see more and more Japanese mushrooms are sold in supermarkets. And here is a quick and easy way of serving them as a tasty side dish.

Serves 4

300g (10½oz) mixed mushrooms, such as shimeji, enoki and shiitake	½ red onion, peeled and thinly sliced	1 tablespoon rice vinegar	½ teaspoon toasted white sesame seeds, to garnish (optional)

Both shimeji and enoki mushrooms come clustered and joined at the base, so cut off and discard the bases and separate the stems. Cut off and discard the stems of the shiitake mushrooms and split the caps in half, by hand.

Bring a saucepan of water to the boil and blanch all the mushrooms and the onion slices for about 3 minutes, then drain. Transfer the mushrooms to a bowl, then add the vinegar, 2 tablespoons of dark soy sauce and 1 teaspoon of toasted sesame oil and mix to incorporate evenly. With the back of a spoon, flatten the surface of the mushroom mixture and leave to stand for 15–20 minutes to marinate.

Divide between four individual serving bowls, garnish with the sesame seeds and serve at room temperature.

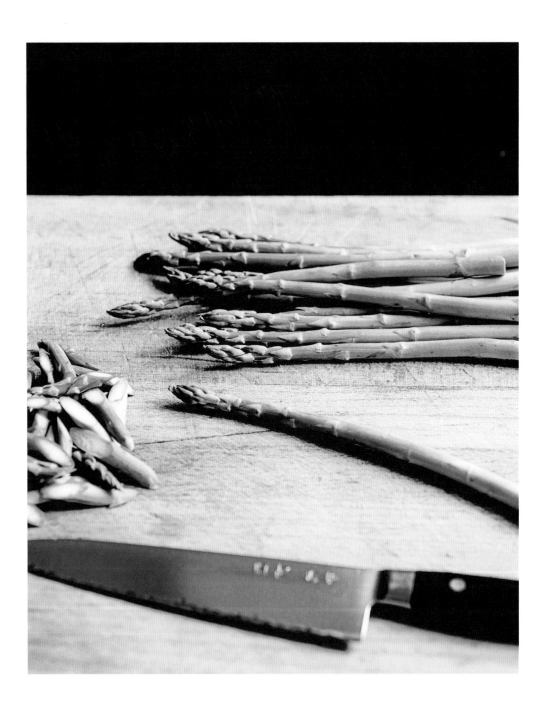

ASPARAGUS WITH WHITE SESAME DRESSING

Dutch traders first introduced asparagus to Japan as an ornamental plant nearly 200 years ago.

Serves 4

12 asparagus spears	2 tablespoons White Sesame Dressing (*see* page 150)

Hold one asparagus spear between your hands and bend until it snaps, then discard the lower end. Repeat the process with the remaining asparagus spears. Cut each spear into 4–5cm (1½–2in) long pieces. Put the asparagus pieces in a medium-sized mixing bowl, sprinkle 1 teaspoon of salt over and gently rub them together with your hands.

Bring a saucepan of water to the boil, add the asparagus, parboil for 2–3 minutes and then drain. Plunge the spears into a bowl of iced water, then drain. Pat them dry with kitchen paper.

Put the asparagus in a mixing bowl, add the white sesame dressing and toss. Divide between four individual serving bowls and serve.

COOK'S TIP

If you are storing fresh asparagus for a few days, wrap in damp newspaper and stand upright in the refrigerator.

OKRA IN SESAME VINEGAR WITH NORI
[OKURA NO NORI-GOMASU AE]

Okura, okra, originates in Africa and is known to have been cultivated in ancient Egypt. It became popular in Japan around the 1960s. Its characteristic stickiness derives from pectin, which helps to regulate healthy digestion as well as lowering cholesterol and blood pressure.

Serves 4

200g (7oz) okra	2 tablespoons Sesame Vinegar (*see* page 157)	1 sheet of nori, crushed into small pieces

Bring a saucepan of water to the boil. Lay the okra on a chopping board and sprinkle with 1 teaspoon of salt. Gently roll them around with your hands – this gets rid of fluff and preserves the colour. Parboil in the pan of water for 2–3 minutes, then drain and immediately plunge into a bowl of iced water and drain. Pat dry thoroughly with kitchen paper.

Cut and discard the stem ends, then chop into about 5mm (¼in) thick slices. In a medium-sized non-metallic bowl, mix the okra with chopsticks or a fork until it becomes sticky, then add the sesame vinegar and 2 teaspoons of dark soy sauce and mix well to combine. Add the crushed nori pieces and lightly mix just before serving.

MUSHROOM RICE [KINOKO-GOHAN]

This is a more economical adaptation of a recipe that usually includes a luxury mushroom called *matsutake*, literally pine-mushroom. These are highly fragrant and expensive fungi – Japan's equivalent of white truffle.

Serves 4

✳	✳	✳	✳	✳
300g (10½oz) short-grain rice	100g (3½oz) shimeji or maitake mushrooms	50g (1¾oz) enoki mushrooms	4 shiitake mushrooms	1 tablespoon sake

Wash the rice (*see* page 167) and set aside to drain in a colander for 30 minutes.

Cut and discard the bases of the shimeji or maitake and enoki mushrooms and separate the clumps with your hands. Cut off and discard the stems of the shiitake and slice the caps.

Put the rice in a heavy-based saucepan with 300ml (½ pint) of water. Add the sake, 1 tablespoon of light soy sauce and ½ teaspoon of salt and stir. Place the mushrooms on top of the rice and cover with the lid. Cook the rice as on page 167.

Fluff and mix the rice when cooked, then serve.

SWEET-SIMMERED BROAD BEANS

In Japanese, broad bean is known as *soramame*, literally sky bean, because its pod grows upward to the sky. It is eaten simmered or deep-fried as an accompanying dish, or dried then deep-fried as a snack.

Serves 4

✺	✺	✺	✺	✺
1.2kg (2lb 10oz) broad beans in pod or 400g (14oz) frozen baby broad beans	2 tablespoons sake	2 tablespoons mirin	2 tablespoons white caster or granulated sugar	1 tablespoon cornflour mixed with 1 tablespoon cold water

Fresh broad beans in pods typically yield only a quarter of their weight when shelled. Shell the broad beans and remove their skins – this is fiddly but the result is well worth the extra effort. Or alternatively, use frozen baby broad beans.

Bring 500ml (18fl oz) of water to the boil with ½ teaspoon of salt over a medium heat, add the beans and cook for 3–5 minutes. Add 1 tablespoon of light soy sauce and all the remaining ingredients, except the cornflour mixture, and let it return to just below the boil. Reduce the heat to low and simmer for about 3 minutes. Stir in the cornflour mixture and simmer for 1–3 minutes or until the sauce thickens.

Remove from the heat, divide between four individual bowls with some of the cooking juices and serve.

FIVE COLOURS IN VINEGAR
[G O S H I K I   N A M A S U]

Namasu is one of the oldest dishes in Japanese cooking. Fruits and vegetables (plus raw meat and fish for non-vegans) are cut into thin strips and mixed with vinegar-based dressings. Dried persimmons are a winter delicacy in Japan, but you can use almost any dried fruit instead, such as apricots, figs or prunes.

Serves 4

❇	❇	❇	❇	❇	❇
2 dried persimmons or dried apricots, figs or prunes	100g (3½oz) daikon (giant white radish), peeled	1 medium carrot, peeled	100g (3½oz) fine green beans, trimmed	4 shiitake mushrooms	100ml (3½fl oz) Three-flavour Vinegar (*see* page 156)

Cut the dried persimmons or other dried fruit into julienne strips. Cut the radish and carrot into julienne strips about 4cm (1½in) long.

Put the beans on a chopping board and sprinkle over some salt. Using flattened hands, roll the beans around a few times – this will help to tenderize them as well as retain the fresh green colour when cooked.

Parboil each vegetable separately in lightly salted boiling water – green beans for 3 minutes, radish and carrot for 2 minutes. Then rinse in cold water, drain thoroughly and pat dry with kitchen paper. Set aside.

Preheat the grill to high.

Cut off and discard the stalks of the shiitake and grill the caps for 1 minute on each side. Slice thinly.

Put the dried fruit, vegetables and mushrooms in a mixing bowl, then pour the vinegar over and toss.

To serve, divide the mixture into four equal portions and lightly squeeze each portion before arranging neatly into mounds in individual serving dishes.

GRILLED AUBERGINE WITH SEASONED MISO [NASU-DENGAKU]

The rather bland, spongy flesh of aubergine is another ideal canvas for the robust dengaku miso. As aubergines found in the West tend to be much bigger than their Japanese counterparts, I allow half per person.

Serves 4

✳	✳	✳	✳	✳
4 tablespoons miso (any colour	4 tablespoons mirin	4 tablespoons white caster or granulated sugar	2 aubergines	2 teaspoons poppy seeds, to garnish

Preheat the grill to high.

Mix the miso, mirin, sugar and 2 tablespoons of dark soy sauce together in a bowl until the sugar is dissolved.

Leave the stems on the aubergines, as they look attractive, and cut in half lengthways. Prick the aubergines skins all over and score the cut surface in a criss-cross pattern (this will help them soak up the miso topping).

Heat 2 tablespoons of vegetable oil in a large frying pan over a medium heat and cook the aubergines, cut-side down, for 8–10 minutes, or until tender. Turn them over, spread the miso on the cut side, sprinkle with the poppy seeds to garnish and place under the grill for 2–3 minutes, until lightly browned. Serve warm.

LEEKS IN GINGER MISO

Japanese use several different types of spring onions and this recipe is based on one using *naga-negi*, long-onion, or sometimes called *shiro-negi*, white-onion, and as the names suggest it has a longer white part. The nearest equivalent outside Japan is leeks. Pickled ginger is typically served as a digestive condiment.

Serves 4

2 young leeks, cleaned and trimmed	2 tablespoons medium-coloured miso	1 teaspoon white caster or granulated sugar	1 tablespoon rice vinegar	1 tablespoon sushi ginger, finely chopped

Cut the leeks diagonally into 5–6mm (¼in) thick rings. Put the leeks in a saucepan, just cover with water and bring to the boil over a medium heat. Reduce the heat to low and simmer for 10–12 minutes.

Meanwhile, mix the remaining ingredients with 1 tablespoon of dark soy sauce in a bowl.

Turn off the heat and drain the leeks briefly so that they are still quite wet, then return to the saucepan. Add the ginger miso and mix well.

Divide into four equal portions and serve warm.

CAULIFLOWER AND BROCCOLI IN MUSTARD MISO

Seasoned miso adds extra taste and flavour to what can otherwise be rather bland boiled vegetables.

Serves 4

200g (7oz) cauliflower	200g (7oz) broccoli	2 teaspoons wholegrain mustard	4 tablespoons white or light-coloured miso	1 teaspoon white caster or granulated sugar	2 tablespoons rice vinegar

Cut the cauliflower and broccoli into large, bite-sized chunks.

Bring a saucepan of lightly salted water to the boil over a high heat and add the cauliflower. Wait for the water to return to the boil before adding the broccoli to blanch for 1 minute. Drain.

For the mustard miso, mix the mustard, miso, sugar and rice vinegar together in a large bowl. Add the vegetables and mix to coat evenly. Divide into four portions and serve warm or at room temperature.

TOFU AND WAKAME MISO SOUP
[TOFU TO WAKAME NO MISO-SHIRU]

Among countless variations of miso soups this is an absolute classic, especially for breakfast. You could consider it Japan's equivalent of Marmite on toast.

Serves 4

✺	✺	✺	✺	✺
20g (¾oz) dried wakame	200g (7oz) tofu (either silken or firm)	1 heaped tablespoon light-coloured miso	1 heaped tablespoon medium-coloured miso	2 spring onions, finely chopped on the diagonal, to garnish

Soak the dried wakame in 4 tablespoons of warm water for 10–15 minutes and drain.

Meanwhile, to drain the tofu, wrap it in kitchen paper, microwave (800W) for 2 minutes, then cut into 1cm (½in) cubes.

Pour 800ml (28fl oz) of Primary Dashi, Secondary Dashi or Vegetarian Dashi (*see* pages 143–147) into a saucepan and bring to the boil over a medium-high heat. Put the miso pastes in a small bowl and mix well, then add a ladleful of dashi from the pot to soften.

The soup must be served hot, so warm four soup bowls with hot (not boiling) water.

Add the wakame, tofu and miso mixture to the pan and let the soup return to the boil for a few seconds, then turn off the heat immediately. (Never let the miso soup reach a rapid boil as it will spoil the flavour.)

Ladle into the warmed bowls, garnish with the spring onions and serve immediately.

ALTERNATIVE FLAVOURINGS
Tofu and *abura-age* (deep-fried tofu), with chopped spring onions
Tofu and shiitake mushrooms with cress
Tofu and mangetout
Tofu and broccoli with ground white or black sesame seeds

GRILLED AUBERGINE MISO SOUP
[YAKINASU NO MISO-SHIRU]

A rich and smoky-flavoured soup, which lends itself well to being served in shallow, Western-style soup bowls.

Serves 4

✳	✳	✳	✳
2 aubergines	3 tablespoons white miso	1 tablespoon dark or red miso	English mustard, to serve

Preheat the grill to the highest setting.

Prick the aubergines with a fork and grill until the skin is blackened all over, turning occasionally until cooked through. Remove from the grill and allow the aubergines to cool. Peel off the blackened skin and cut the flesh into large, bite-sized pieces. Set aside and keep warm.

The soup must be served hot, so warm four soup bowls with hot (not boiling) water.

Pour 600ml (20fl oz) of Primary Dashi (*see* page 143) into a pan over a medium heat and bring to just below the boil, then reduce the heat to low and maintain the temperature.

Put the miso pastes in a bowl and mix to blend, then add a ladleful of dashi from the saucepan and stir to soften the pastes. Add the mixture back into the saucepan, bring to the boil and immediately turn off the heat.

Arrange the aubergine pieces in the centre of the warmed soup bowls. Gently ladle in the soup around the aubergines, put a small dab of mustard on the top of each portion and serve.

FINE BEAN IN BLACK SESAME DRESSING
[INGEN NO KURO-GOMA AE]

Compared to white sesame seeds, black ones have a stronger flavour and therefore, dark or normal soy sauce can be used.

Serves 4

100g (3½oz) fine green beans	4 tablespoons toasted black sesame seeds	1 teaspoon white caster or granulated sugar

Cut the beans into 3–4cm (1¼–1½in) lengths. Blanch them in plenty of lightly salted boiling water for 2–3 minutes. Rinse in cold water, drain and pat dry with kitchen paper. Put the beans in a bowl, then add 2 tablespoons of dark soy sauce and, with your hands, mix and lightly squeeze.

To make the black sesame dressing, put the toasted sesame seeds and sugar in a *suribachi*, a Japanese mortar, and grind to form a coarse paste – do not overgrind them; leave some seeds still visible. Add 1 tablespoon of dark soy sauce and mix well.

Transfer the beans to a separate bowl, then add the black sesame dressing and mix well to coat each bean. Divide into four equal portions and serve in piles in individual dishes.

RICE COOKED WITH FRESH PEAS
[E N D Ō - G O H A N]

A bowl of plump green peas among glistening white rice not only looks beautiful but is also a tasty new-season arrival.

Serves 4

✵	✵	✵
300g (10½oz) short-grain rice	200g (7oz) fresh peas in pods (or about 100g/3½oz podded peas)	2 teaspoons mirin

Wash the rice (see page 167) and set aside to drain in a colander for 30 minutes.

Shell the peas, rinse under cold running water and drain.

Put the rice, peas and 360ml (12½fl oz) of water in a heavy-based saucepan with the mirin and 1 teaspoon of salt, and stir once. Cook as on page 167. Fluff the rice and serve.

VARIATION
Use frozen edamame beans instead of peas.

TERIYAKI TOFU STEAKS

A mild taste of tofu is like having a blank canvas for a cook to create any culinary painting.

Serves 4

✳	✳	✳	✳	✳	✳	✳
600g (1lb 5oz) firm cotton tofu, cut into 4 equal rectangles	2 tablespoons plain flour, for dusting	4 tablespoons sake	6 tablespoons mirin	200g (7oz) daikon (giant white radish)	½ teaspoon *shichimi-tōgarashi* (seven-spice chilli powder) or chilli powder	a handful of cress, to garnish

Drain the tofu by following one of the methods in the tip below. Dust the tofu with the flour.

Heat 1 tablespoon of vegetable oil in a frying pan over a medium heat and add the tofu. Cook for 3–5 minutes until light brown and crisp on one side, then turn over to cook the other side for a further 3 minutes. Pour in the sake, mirin and 2 tablespoons of dark soy sauce and simmer for 5–7 minutes, uncovered.

Meanwhile, peel and grate the radish and drain slightly in a sieve – it should yield about 4–5 heaped tablespoons of grated radish. Add the grated radish to the pan, stir and then let the cooking juices return to just boiling.

Place the tofu on individual dishes, spoon over the teriyaki sauce mix from the pan and sprinkle over the *shichimi-tōgarashi*. Garnish with the cress and serve.

COOK'S TIP
Here are five different ways to drain tofu:
Natural method Leave to stand on a slightly angled chopping board or a flat bamboo tray for 15–20 minutes.
Boiling method Boil a whole block for 5–10 minutes or for 2–3 minutes in smaller pieces.
Microwave Wrap in kitchen paper and microwave (600–800W) for 3 minutes.
Squeezing method Wrap the tofu in a clean damp muslin cloth and squeeze.
Pressing method Sandwich the tofu between two boards, slightly angled, with or without a weight and leave for 10–15 minutes.

COMFORT

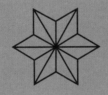

SOBA WITH DUCK IN HOT BROTH
[KAMO NAMBAN]

This is one of the most popular classic soba dishes, I have made a slight change to it by substituting Japanese white spring onions (which are difficult to find outside of Japan) with young leeks.

Serves 2

✳	✳	✳	✳	✳
1 duck breast, skin on	1 tender young leek, cleaned and trimmed	600ml (20fl oz) soup broth (300ml/½ pint All-purpose Noodle Sauce, *see* page 152, mixed with 300ml/½ pint water)	200g (7oz) dried soba noodles	*shichimi-tōgarashi* (seven-spice chilli powder – optional)

Trim the duck breast of excess fat and prick the skin with a fork. Heat a saucepan over a medium heat and wipe the inside base with a clean, cold damp cloth (this stops the meat from sticking). Place the breast, skin-side down, in the pan and cook for 3–5 minutes, then turn over and cook for a further 3 minutes. Remove from the heat and rinse under running hot water to wash off any remaining fat. Put the breast on a chopping board to rest. Wipe the saucepan clean with kitchen paper.

Halve the leek lengthways and cut diagonally into thin slices.

Cut the duck into 3–5mm (⅛–¼in) thick slices. Put the duck and leek in the cleaned saucepan with the soup broth and bring to the boil while skimming off any scum that floats to the surface, and simmer for 5–6 minutes.

Meanwhile, cook the noodles as on page 164.

Divide the noodles between two warmed bowls. Ladle in the hot broth mixture, arrange the duck slices on top, sprinkle with *shichimi-tōgarashi*, if using, and serve immediately.

SALT-SALMON AND RICE
[SAKE-CHAZUKE]

Salt-salmon, *shiozake,* is possibly one of my favourite and most used ingredients. There is always a jar of *shiozake* flakes in my refrigerator, ready to be used for a quick *ochazuke*, rice ball filling, in salads, or with noodles. It is highly versatile and cunningly easy to make and keeps for a couple of weeks refrigerated, though it always gets eaten before then. When I was a small child, upon seeing a whole salmon or yellowtail hanging under the eaves of my grandparents' house, I used to wonder how cold air and salt could turn the fish even more delicious.

Serves 4

4 portions of cooked rice, about 140g (5oz) each, hot or cold	8 heaped tablespoons Salt-salmon Flakes (*see* page 155)	4 tablespoons toasted and ground white sesame seeds	2 teaspoons wasabi paste	4 cups of hot green tea of your choice, to serve

Put each portion of rice in a separate bowl, place 2 heaped tablespoons of salt-salmon flakes on top of each portion, scatter 1 tablespoon of sesame seeds over, then place a dab of wasabi paste on top. Pour four cups of hot tea and serve alongside the salt-salmon and rice.

BEEF ON RICE [GYŪDON]

This is another popular *donburi* dish, especially among the young. There is a fast-food chain company that boasts an impressive growth record and is listed on the Tokyo Stock Exchange serving just this single item.

Serves 4

✳	✳	✳	✳	✳
400g (14oz) thinly sliced beef steak, such as minute steak	2 medium onions, thinly sliced	80ml (3fl oz) mirin	2 tablespoons grated fresh ginger	800g (1lb 12oz) freshly cooked rice, hot

Pound the beef with the back of a heavy knife or rolling pin to flatten, then cut into paper-thin 5cm (2in) length pieces.

Heat 1 tablespoon of vegetable oil in a saucepan over a high heat and stir-fry the onions for a few minutes. Add the beef and stir-fry until it is just turning brown, then pour in 200ml (7fl oz) of water, the mirin and 80ml (3fl oz) of dark soy sauce, and bring to the boil. Remove from the heat and add the grated ginger.

Divide the hot rice between four warmed *donburi* or deep soup bowls. With a large spoon, scoop one portion of the beef mixture and sauce on top of each portion of rice and serve immediately.

MOON UDON [TSUKIMI UDON]

Tsukimi, which literally means "moon viewing" in Japanese, is a genteel pastime in autumn when the air is clear and the moon is full. Here, the whole yellow egg yolk in the centre is depicted as the full moon surrounded by semi-cooked egg white and noodles as clouds. Choose the freshest eggs you can find.

Serves 2

❋	❋	❋	❋	❋	❋	❋
200g (7oz) dried udon noodles	300ml (½ pint) All-purpose Noodle Sauce (*see* page 152)	2 tablespoons mirin	4 slices of *kamaboko*, fish paste cake (optional)	2 very fresh eggs	1 spring onion, finely chopped, to garnish	*shichimi-tōgarashi* (seven-spice chilli powder), to serve (optional)

Cook the noodles as on page 164 and portion between two warmed bowls. Keep warm. Preheating the bowls is particularly important for this recipe as you need all the retained heat to semi-cook the eggs.

Meanwhile, heat the noodle sauce and mirin in a saucepan with 400ml (14fl oz) of water to just below boiling. Pour half a ladleful of hot broth over each noodle mound and keep the rest on a simmer.

If including *kamaboko*, arrange 2 slices at the side of the noodles. With the back of a ladle, make a hollowed nest in the centre of the noodles. Crack an egg and gently place the whole egg in the nest and ladle the remaining broth around it, then immediately cover each bowl with clingfilm to "poach" the egg for 1 minute. The egg white should turn opaque white from the heat of the broth, but if you prefer the egg more cooked, microwave (800W) for 10–12 seconds.

Remove the clingfilm, garnish with the chopped spring onion and a sprinkle of *shichimi-tōgarashi*, if liked, and serve immediately.

SEA BREAM RICE [TAI-MESHI]

This is one of the most celebrated rice dishes of all, which is not surprising as it combines two of Japan's most popular ingredients – rice and sea bream. Traditionally, a whole handsome fish is cooked in a *donabe*, a lidded clay casserole, and brought to the table. In this version, the fish is grilled separately and added later for serving and eating.

Serves 4

300g (10½oz) short-grain rice	2 tablespoons sake	400g (14oz) sea bream fillet, skin on	1 tablespoon finely julienned fresh ginger

Wash and drain the rice (*see* page 167), then place it in a heavy-based saucepan with 300ml (½ pint) of Primary or Secondary Dashi (*see* pages 143 and 144), the sake and 2 tablespoons of light soy sauce. Leave to stand for 10 minutes.

Cut the fish into 5mm (¼in) thick bite-sized pieces by holding the knife at a 30° angle so that the blade is almost horizontal to the fillet. Transfer to a flat bamboo basket or a paper-lined plate, then gently rub 1 teaspoon of salt on the skin side and leave to stand for 5–8 minutes. Pat dry with kitchen paper.

Preheat the grill to high and grill the fish for 5 minutes on each side.

Cook the rice over a medium heat, then when it reaches the boil and steam begins to rise, reduce the heat to low and quickly place the fish, skin-side up, on top of the rice, cover immediately and continue to cook until the steam stops. Turn off the heat and quickly scatter over the ginger, cover again and steam for a further 10 minutes before serving.

CHICKEN AND MISO PORRIDGE
[T O R I   M I S O - Z Ō S U I]

This dish has a plenty of flavour from the chicken and miso – think of it as a Japanese risotto.

Serves 4

✳	✳	✳	✳	✳
600g (1lb 5oz) cooked rice	200g (7oz) skinless chicken thigh fillets	4 tablespoons sake	8 tablespoons medium-coloured miso	4 spring onions, finely chopped on the diagonal

If you are using leftover rice, put it in a large sieve and rinse under hot running water to wash off the starch and drain. Cut the chicken into thin, bite-sized pieces and mix in a bowl with the sake.

Put 1.2 litres (2 pints) of Dashi of your choice (see pages 143–147) and 2 tablespoons of dark soy sauce in a saucepan and bring to the boil over a medium heat, then add the chicken mixture. Reduce the heat to a simmer, skimming off any scum that floats to the surface, and cook for 5–7 minutes.

Put the miso in a small bowl and add a ladleful of the broth to soften, then pour the mixture into the pan. Add the rice, then let it return to a simmer and cook for a further 3–5 minutes. Scatter the spring onions over and remove from the heat.

Divide between four warmed bowls and serve immediately.

JAPANESE-STYLE RÖSTI WITH SOY PORK

Here is a Swiss classic with a Japanese twist.

Serves 4

✳	✳	✳	✳	✳
400g (14oz) pork loin, roughly chopped	4 tablespoons sake	600g (1lb 5oz) waxy potatoes (such as Maris Peer or Desirée), peeled	2 teaspoons cornflour	12 French breakfast radishes, cleaned and trimmed

Put the pork in a bowl with the sake and 4 tablespoons of dark soy sauce. Leave to marinate for 10–15 minutes.

Shred the potatoes with a Japanese mandoline or a grater over a large bowl of cold water and then rinse away any excess starch. Drain the shreds and spread over a clean tea towel, then roll up and press gently to blot away excess water. Unroll the tea towel and put the shreds in a large bowl with 2 tablespoons of vegetable oil and mix.

Squeeze the pork of any excess marinade and coat with the cornflour.

Heat 2 tablespoons of vegetable oil in a 24cm (9½in) non-stick frying pan over a medium heat and spread over half the potato shreds. Spread the pork evenly over the first layer, then cover with the rest of the potato, as evenly as possible.

Drizzle a further 2 tablespoons of vegetable oil over the rösti and turn over after 15–20 minutes or when the base has become golden and crisp. You can either flip it like a pancake (if you are brave enough) or by placing a similar diameter plate over the pan, turn it over, then carefully slide the rosti back into the pan to cook the other side for 12–15 minutes.

Remove from the pan on to a chopping board. Sprinkle with some salt and cut into four, then serve with 3 radishes each.

EGG AND CHIVE PORRIDGE
[NIRATAMA-ZŌSUI]

My mother used to make me this comforting and tasty dish whenever I was beginning to come down with a cold. It is warming and reviving, yet easy to digest. Chinese chives are deep green and flat-leaved and sold in Asian grocery shops.

Serves 4

600g (1lb 5oz) cooked rice	4 tablespoons sake	100g (3½oz) Chinese chives, cut into 3–4cm (1¼–1½in) lengths	4 eggs, beaten

If you are using leftover rice, put it in a large sieve and rinse under hot running water to wash off the starch and drain.

Put 1.2 litres (2 pints) of Dashi of your choice (see pages 143–147), the sake, 4 tablespoons of light soy sauce and 2–3 teaspoons of salt in a saucepan and bring to the boil over a medium heat. Add the chives, then reduce the heat and simmer for 5–7 minutes.

Add the rice and return to a simmer over a medium heat. Then drizzle the beaten eggs over the rice; do not stir, but immediately cover and remove from the heat. The eggs will cook in the residual heat of the pot but still be soft and runny.

Divide between four warmed bowls and serve immediately with spoons. The secret of this dish is to eat it while it is still hot and the eggs are soft.

ROAST PUMPKIN GINGER MASH

Kabocha, pumpkin, has a naturally sweet taste, which is further enhanced by roasting.
This side dish goes particularly well with rich roast meats.

Serves 4

1.2kg (2lb 10oz) unpeeled pumpkin, quartered and deseeded	30g (1oz) unsalted butter, softened	1 teaspoon finely grated fresh ginger	ground white pepper

Preheat the oven to 200°C/400°F/gas mark 6.

Mix 1 tablespoon of vegetable oil with 1 teaspoon of toasted sesame oil. Brush the inside
of the pumpkin with the oil mixture, then sprinkle 1 teaspoon of sea salt over it. Place
the pumpkin, skin-side down, in a roasting tray and roast for 50–60 minutes or until
very tender.

Scoop the pumpkin flesh from the skin and put in a bowl. Add the butter and mash until
very smooth. Add 1 tablespoon of light soy sauce and the ginger, then season to taste
with salt and ground white pepper. Serve warm.

LAMB STEAKS WITH GRILLED AUBERGINE

Here I have matched a traditional Japanese method of preparing and smoking aubergines with lamb, a meat not often seen on the Japanese table. The smoky flavour of the aubergine is perfectly paired with the strong-flavoured lamb. The number of aubergines is based on average-sized aubergines found in the West, so adjust the amount if you are able to source smaller, slender ones that are similar to those sold in Japan.

Serves 4

2 aubergines	1 tablespoon rice vinegar	1 teaspoon grated fresh ginger	4 x 200g (7oz) lamb steaks	*shichimi-tōgarashi* (seven-spice chilli powder)	freshly ground black pepper

Preheat the grill to high.

Prick the aubergines with the tip of a knife or a skewer, then place under the grill and cook for 15 minutes, turning regularly until the skin is blackened and wrinkled and the flesh feels soft to the touch. Put them in a plastic bag, seal and leave until cool enough to touch. With a bamboo skewer inserted just beneath the skin, slide along the length of the aubergines to remove all the blackened skin. Cut the aubergine into 4cm (1½in) long pieces and put in a bowl.

For the soy-ginger sauce, combine the rice vinegar and ginger with 2 tablespoons of dark soy sauce, then pour this over the aubergines and mix to coat. Cover with foil to keep warm and set aside.

Heat 1 tablespoon of vegetable oil and ½ teaspoon of sesame oil in a large frying pan over a medium-high heat. Season the lamb with chilli powder and salt and pepper, then cook on each side for 2 minutes for rare or a little longer if preferred. Transfer the lamb to a chopping board and loosely cover with foil to keep warm, then rest for 5 minutes. Cut the steaks into large, diagonal bite-sized slices.

Divide and arrange the lamb and aubergines between four individual serving plates. Drizzle over any remaining sauce from the aubergines and serve.

DEEP-FRIED SCALLOPS IN RICE CRACKERS
[HOTATE NO ARARE-TATSUTA-AGE]

In *Tatsuta-age*, food is usually marinated first then coated with cornflour or plain flour, but in this version rice crackers do both jobs of seasoning and coating. You can use any soy-flavoured rice crackers, but my favourite choice is *kaki-no-tane*, small peppery ones that look like seeds.

Serves 4

8 sweet chestnuts	100g (3½oz) *kaki-no-tane* (rice crackers)	200g (7oz) shelled scallops without roe	2 tablespoons plain flour	2 egg whites, lightly beaten

Start by blanching the chestnuts in boiling water for 10–15 minutes to soften the skins, then peel both the outer skin and bitter pellicle.

Put the rice crackers in a plastic bag and lightly crush them with a rolling pin to crumble (do not overdo this as what you want is crunchy broken pieces not powdered crackers). Transfer the cracker crumble to a dish.

Lightly dust the scallops with the flour. Dip in the egg white to moisten, then roll in the cracker crumbs to coat.

Heat 1–1.5 litres (1¾–2¾ pints) of vegetable oil to 160°C (325°F) in a large, deep frying pan and deep-fry the chestnuts for 5–8 minutes – they will sink to the bottom initially and slowly rise to the top. Turn them a few times. Remove and drain on a wire rack or kitchen paper.

Heat the oil to 170°C (340°F) and deep-fry the scallops in small batches for 3–5 minutes – they will sink to the middle of the oil and rise to the surface. Turn them once. Take one out to test – it should be slightly undercooked in the middle. Remove and drain on a wire rack.

Divide into four equal portions and put on individual serving plates, place 2 chestnuts on each and serve.

PLAICE IN PARCEL
[HIRAME NO HOIRU-YAKI]

Cooking fish wrapped in foil is a gentle, forgiving method and no washing up! All the flavours are enveloped until the diner opens the parcel. This is a particularly suitable way of cooking delicately flavoured fish.

Serves 4

4 x 200g (7oz) plaice or sole fillets	butter, for greasing	4 pak choi, halved lengthways	4 shiitake mushrooms, stems discarded	4 thick lemon slices	4 tablespoons sake

Start by salting the fish with 2 teaspoons of sea salt and leave it to stand for 20–30 minutes.

Meanwhile, preheat the oven to 200°C/400°F/gas mark 6. Butter the centre of four 30cm (12in) foil squares.

Pat the fish dry with kitchen paper and place on the buttered part of the foil square. Put the pak choi and shiitake next to the fish, the lemon slices on top and then drizzle sake over the arrangement. Fold the foil into a parcel allowing as much headroom as possible and seal the ends tightly. Place the parcels on a large baking tray and cook in the oven for 12–15 minutes.

Put the parcels on individual plates, bring to the table and let each diner open their parcel.

COOK'S TIP
This method can be adapted for almost any white flesh fish, or shelled scallops.

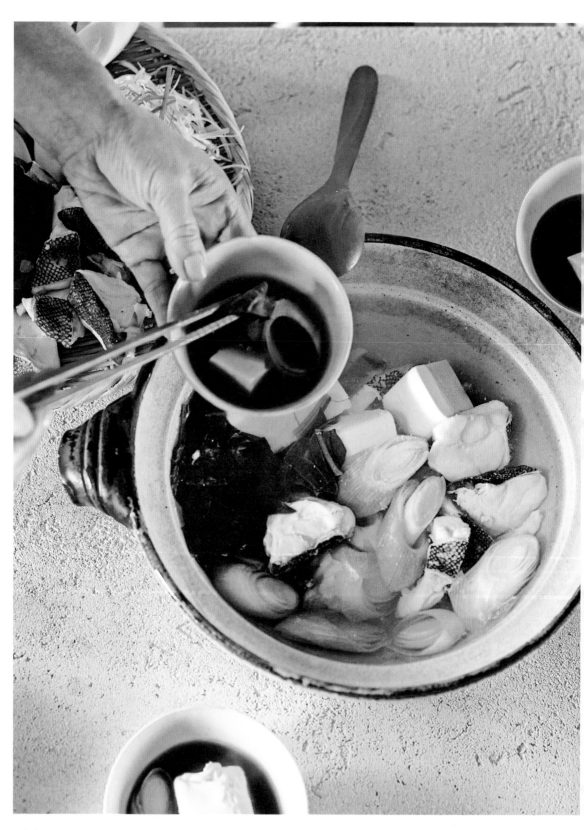

COD HOTPOT [TARA-CHIRI-NABE]

This is one of the standard Japanese hotpot dishes eaten in winter. In order to fully enjoy cod's understated taste, keep the other ingredients simple.

Serves 4

✵	✵	✵	✵	✵	✵	✵
2 postcard-sized pieces of dried kelp	100ml (3½fl oz) sake	600g (1lb 5oz) cod fillet, cut into large, bite-sized chunks	400g (14oz) soft silken tofu	200g (7oz) leeks, clean, trimmed and cut into 1cm (½in) thick diagonal slices	4 spring onions	200g (7oz) spinach, roughly chopped

To prepare the cooking broth, put 1.2 litres (2 pints) of water in a casserole or a large saucepan with the kelp and sake, then leave to infuse for 30 minutes.

Meanwhile, sprinkle 1 teaspoon salt over the cod and leave to stand for 10 minutes. Blanch the cod in boiling water for 1–2 minutes or until the colour begins to turn translucent, then transfer into iced water and drain.

Cut the tofu into 3cm (1¼in) squares and leave in cold water for about 10 minutes, then drain – this prevents the tofu from clouding the cooking broth.

Heat the broth over a medium-high heat and bring to the boil. When it begins to boil, remove the kelp, add the cod and leeks, return to the boil and skim off any scum that floats to the surface. Reduce the heat to low, cover with a lid and simmer for 10 minutes.

Meanwhile, cut the spring onions into 5cm (2in) lengths and very finely slice lengthways. Soak in a bowl of cold water for about 10 minutes or until they curl. Drain well.

Add the spinach and tofu to the pot and let the broth return to the boil for 2–3 minutes. Remove from the heat and, using a slotted spoon, divide between four serving bowls, garnish with the spring onion curls and serve with citrus soy vinegar (see page 158) to pour over and *shichimi-tōgarashi* on the side, if you wish.

COOK'S TIPS
Try this recipe with other white-fleshed fish such as sea bream or turbot. Also, why not finish the dinner by adding cooked rice or udon noodles to the broth? There should be about 1 litre (1¾ pints) of broth left in the pot, add about 400g (14oz) cooked rice, return to the boil for a few minutes while stirring and mix, adjust the seasoning with salt and soy sauce to taste and serve. If using noodles, cook 200g (7oz) dried udon noodles as on page 164 and add to the pot. Bring the pot to the boil over a medium heat, cook for 3–5 minutes and adjust the seasoning with mirin and dark soy sauce if required.

THICK-ROLL SUSHI [FUTO-MAKI]

Also called *date-maki*, literally "dandy" roll, because of its colourful fillings, a thick roll typically contains 4–5 cooked ingredients. The rolling technique is the same as in thin rolls (*see* page 19).

Makes 2 rolls (16 slices)

✲	✲	✲	✲	✲	✲	✲
2 sheets of nori	400g (14oz) prepared sushi rice (*see* page 160)	1 carrot, peeled, cut into thick strips and steamed	20g (¾oz) fine green beans, trimmed and lightly steamed	20g (¾oz) prepared shiitake mushroom slices (see below)	½ prepared Dashi-rolled Omelette (*see* page 36), cut into 1 x 20cm (½ x 8in) long strips	20g (¾oz) prepared *kampyō* (dried gourd), cut into 20cm (8in) lengths (*see* opposite)

For each roll, place a sheet of nori, shiny-side down, along the edge of your rolling mat. Moisten your hands in a bowl of mild vinegar water, form two log shapes with half the rice and put them in the centre of the nori. Spread the rice evenly across the whole width of the nori, leaving a 4cm (1½in) border of the sheet furthest from you uncovered.

Lay half the carrot strips across the centre of the rice, followed by half the beans and half the mushrooms on either side. Arrange half the omelette strips and half the *kampyō* on either side of the beans and mushrooms.

To roll, lift up the edge of the mat closest to you with your thumbs and index fingers, keeping the filling in place with your middle and third fingers, and roll the mat over so that the top edge of the nori meets the edge of the rice. Lift the edge of the mat slightly and push the roll away from you so that the uncovered strip of nori seals the roll. Gently but firmly press along the length of the roll using both hands to evenly shape it. Repeat to make the second roll.

Moisten a sharp knife with the vinegar water, and cut each roll in half, then each half into four equal slices, cleaning and moistening the knife before each cut. Arrange on a platter, cut-side up, to show off the centre, and serve with sushi pickled ginger as a garnish if you wish.

HOW TO PREPARE DRIED SHIITAKE MUSHROOMS
Soak 8 dried shiitake mushrooms in just enough warm water to cover for 10 minutes. Drain, reserving the liquid, and cut off and discard the stems. Put the liquid,

mushrooms, 2 tablespoons of mirin, 3 tablespoons of white caster or granulatedsugar and 2 tablespoons of dark soy sauce in a saucepan. Bring to the boil over a medium heat, reduce the heat and simmer for 20–30 minutes, or until the liquid has almost disappeared. Let the mushrooms cool in the saucepan, then squeeze to drain and then cut into thin slices.

HOW TO PREPARE DRIED GOURD STRIPS

Wash 20g (¾oz) *kampyō* in cold water with a scrubbing action. Add 2 tablespoons of salt and continue to rub in the water until soft. Rinse and then soak in fresh water for 2–3 hours. Drain and put in a saucepan with enough water to cover and simmer for 10–15 minutes. Add 500ml (18fl oz) of Dashi of your choice (*see* pages 143–147) with 2 tablespoons of white caster or granulated sugar and 2 tablespoons of dark soy sauce and bring to the boil, then simmer for 10 minutes or until the strips turn golden yellow. Allow to cool in the stock before cutting to desired lengths.

SWEET

TOKYO ROLL

This is a Japanese variation on the Swiss roll.

Serves 6–8

✻	✻	✻	✻	✻	✻	✻
100g (3½oz) caster sugar, plus extra for dusting and dredging	100g (3½oz) plain flour, plus extra for dusting	10g (¼oz) matcha (green tea powder)	4 large eggs	200ml (7fl oz) double cream	100g (3½oz) *koshi-an* (smooth sweet adzuki bean paste)	icing sugar, for dusting

Preheat the oven to 180°C/350°F/gas mark 4. Grease and line a 33 x 23cm (13 x 9in) Swiss roll tin with nonstick baking paper. Dust with a half-and-half mixture of caster sugar and flour.

Mix the flour with the green tea powder and sift 2–3 times.

Put the eggs and sugar in a bowl, place over a pan of simmering water and whisk, using an electric hand whisk, until pale, creamy and thick enough to leave a trail on the surface when the whisk is lifted.

Remove the egg mixture from the heat, then sift half the green tea-flour mixture over and gently fold in with a metal spoon. Repeat with the remaining green tea-flour mixture, then lightly stir in 1 tablespoon of hot water.

Pour the mixture into the prepared tin, then tilt the tin backwards and forwards to spread the mixture evenly. Bake for 10–12 minutes, until well risen and firm to the touch.

Meanwhile, place a large sheet of greaseproof paper on top of a clean, damp tea towel. Dredge the paper thickly with caster sugar.

Working quickly, turn out the sponge on to the paper, trim off the crusty edges and let it cool down. While the cake is cooling down, whisk the cream until soft peaks form. Spread the cream over the cake and make a line of adzuki bean paste along the long edge nearest to you.

Roll up the cake, starting from the long edge with the paste on, with the aid of the paper. Make the first turn firmly so that the whole cake will roll evenly and have a good shape when finished, but roll more lightly after the first turn. Place the cake, seam-side down, on a chopping board, dust with icing sugar, then slice and serve.

MT FUJI

An adaptation of the famous French dessert, Mont Blanc, using meringues and sweet adzuki bean paste.

Serves 4

✳	✳	✳	✳	✳	✳	✳
2 large egg whites (approx 80g/2¾oz in weight)	110g (3¾oz) caster sugar, plus 1 tablespoon for the topping	200g (7oz) mascarpone cheese	200ml (7fl oz) low-fat fromage frais	1 teaspoon matcha (green tea powder)	4 tablespoons sweet adzuki bean paste	icing sugar, for dusting

Preheat the oven to 150°C/300°F/gas mark 2. Line a baking sheet with nonstick baking paper.

For the meringues, put the egg whites in a clean stainless steel or copper mixing bowl, and whisk, using an electric hand whisk, on a low speed for 2–3 minutes until foamy. Increase the speed to medium and whisk for a further minute. Increase to high and continue whisking until the whites are stiff, then begin adding the caster sugar, a dessertspoonful at a time, until the mixture is stiff and glossy.

Spoon four heaped tablespoons on to the lined baking sheet, spacing them evenly. Then, using the back of the spoon, hollow out the centres. Place on the centre shelf of the oven and cook for 30 minutes. Turn off the oven and leave the meringues in the oven until they are completely cool.

For the topping, put the mascarpone, fromage frais and the remaining 1 tablespoon of caster sugar in a bowl and mix until the sugar is completely dissolved. Sift in the green tea powder, then mix until it is evenly combined.

To assemble and finish, first spoon some of the sweet adzuki bean paste into each meringue, top each with some of the mascarpone mixture, then dust with icing sugar and some green tea powder. Serve.

GREEN TEA ICE CREAM

With a hint of bitterness from the matcha, this ice cream not only looks beautifully green but also tastes fresh and rather sophisticated. The powder is sold in a small tin and lasts up to a year, but once opened, keep it refrigerated.

Serves 4–6

300ml (½ pint) semi-skimmed or whole milk	300ml (½ pint) double cream	4 large egg yolks	150g (5½oz) caster sugar	1 tablespoon matcha (green tea powder)	a few mint leaves, to decorate

Follow the same process of making the custard mixture as for Black Sesame Ice Cream (*see* page 133) until just before adding the sesame paste.

In a small bowl, mix the green tea powder with 3 tablespoons of warm water and stir well to form a smooth paste.

Add the tea paste to the custard mixture and stir well until it is completely combined and the colour appears uniformly light green, then set aside to cool.

If you have an ice-cream maker, put the mixture in and follow the manufacturer's instructions. But if you are not using an ice-cream maker, put the mixture in a shallow, plastic container with a lid and place in the freezer, then keep stirring every 30 minutes or so for 3–4 hours, until frozen.

Serve in scoops, decorated with the mint leaves.

BLACK SESAME ICE CREAM

Black sesame seeds give this ice cream a rich, nutty taste and a dramatic dark appearance. It is made easier if you can source the ready-made sesame paste from Japanese or Asian stores.

Serves 4–6

✻	✻	✻	✻	✻	✻	✻
300ml (½ pint) semi-skimmed or whole milk	300ml (½ pint) double cream	4 large egg yolks	150g (5½oz) caster sugar	2 tablespoons black sesame paste (*see* page 135)	1 teaspoon vanilla extract	black sesame seeds, to decorate

For the custard mixture, heat the milk and cream in a medium saucepan over a medium heat to just below the boil.

Put the egg yolks, sugar and ¼ teaspoon of salt in a medium heatproof bowl and whisk until pale. Then slowly begin to pour the hot milk mixture into the yolk mixture while constantly stirring. Do not hurry this process otherwise the eggs may curdle.

Pour the mixture back into the pan and place over a medium-low heat. Cook for 10–12 minutes, stirring the mixture, until it is thick enough to coat the back of the spoon. Add the black sesame paste and vanilla extract, mix well and then set aside to cool completely.

If you have an ice-cream maker, put the mixture in and follow the manufacturer's instructions. But if you are not using an ice-cream maker, put the mixture in a shallow, plastic container with a lid and place in the freezer, then keep stirring every 30 minutes or so for 3–4 hours, until frozen.

Serve in scoops with a sprinkling of sesame seeds to decorate.

JAPANESE IN 7

BLACK SESAME PANNA COTTA

Panna cotta is one of my favourite Italian desserts – here, I've given it a Japanese twist.
You can buy ready-made black sesame paste from Japanese stores, but it is easy to
make with a bit of elbow-grease.

Serves 4

✳	✳	✳	✳	✳	✳
100g (3½oz) black sesame seeds	1 tablespoon clear honey	2 teaspoons powdered gelatine	250ml (9fl oz) whole milk	250ml (9fl oz) double cream	1 tablespoon caster sugar

Start by making the black sesame paste. Dry toast the sesame seeds in a non-stick frying
pan over a medium heat until they start to pop. (They may be sold ready toasted, but
it is worth refreshing them). Immediately transfer the seeds into a *suribachi*, a ribbed
Japanese mortar, and grind for 30–45 minutes or until you have a smooth paste. Add
the honey and continue grinding until evenly mixed. The paste will keep for 3–4 weeks,
refrigerated, in a sterilised jam jar.

To make the panna cotta, put 2 teaspoons of cold water in a small bowl and sprinkle over
the gelatine. Leave to soak for 5–8 minutes.

Meanwhile, put the milk, cream and sugar in a saucepan and heat over a medium heat,
taking care not to let it boil. Add 2 tablespoons of the sesame paste and stir in the soaked
gelatine, mix well, then return just to the boil and simmer for 3–5 minutes.

Remove from the heat and stand for about 10 minutes to cool slightly, then pour into four
individual heatproof glasses. Leave to stand to cool further before placing in the fridge to
chill for 3–4 hours or until set.

VARIATION
Instead of sesame seeds, try this with matcha. Sift a tablespoon of matcha into a bowl
with 2 tablespoons of whole milk and add to the panna cotta mix once it's slightly cooled.
Mix well to ensure it is evenly combined.

MATCHA JELLY

This is an easy yet highly sophisticated and visually stunning dessert.

Serves 4

❋	❋	❋
1 tablespoon matcha (green tea powder)	2 tablespoons granulated sugar	1½ teaspoons agar-agar powder dissolved in 3 teaspoons cold water

Sift the matcha into a medium-sized bowl, then add 50ml (2fl oz) of warm water (about 60°C/140°F) and mix well until there are no lumps. Add the sugar and the agar-agar mixture to the tea, then add another 450ml (16fl oz) of warm water and stir to mix.

Transfer the tea mixture into a saucepan and heat over a medium heat until it reaches just below the boil, then reduce the heat slightly and simmer for 2–3 minutes.

Remove from the heat and cool down a little before dividing between four wine glasses. Let it cool down to room temperature before placing in the refrigerator. Serve chilled.

THREE JAPANESE-STYLE MERINGUES

If you are wondering what to do with leftover egg whites, here is the answer – light and billowy, crisp meringues, Japanese-style.

Makes 12

✳	✳	✳	✳	✳	✳
4 large egg whites, (approx. 160g/5¾oz in weight), at room temperature	220g (8oz) caster sugar	1 tablespoon *kinako* (soybean flour)	1 teaspoon matcha (green tea powder), sifted twice	½ tablespoon black sesame seeds	whipped cream and berries, to serve (optional)

Preheat the oven to 150°C/300°F/gas mark 2. Line three baking sheets with nonstick baking paper.

Put the egg whites in a large, clean stainless steel or copper mixing bowl. Whisk, using an electric hand whisk, on a low speed for 2–3 minutes until the whites become foamy. Increase the speed to medium and whisk for a further minute before increasing the speed again to high until the whites form stiff peaks. Divide the mixture into three portions and put each into a clean mixing bowl. Also divide the caster sugar into three equal portions.

Next, whisk one portion of the sugar into one portion of egg whites, on high speed, about a dessertspoonful at a time, until the mixture becomes stiff and glossy, then set aside.

Sift the soybean flour into the second portion of sugar, then mix and sift the whole mixture again. Now whisk this sugar into the second bowl of egg whites, on high speed, as before and set aside.

Clean and dry the beaters. Mix the matcha into the last portion of sugar and sift the whole mixture once more to ensure an even mixture. Whisk this tea mixture into the third portion of egg whites on high speed as before.

Spoon four heaped dessertspoons of each meringue mixture onto the baking sheets, spacing them generously apart. Sprinkle the sesame seeds on top of the plain meringues. Bake in the middle of the oven for about 1 hour until the meringues sound crisp when tapped underneath. Turn off the oven and leave the meringues in the oven until completely cooled.

Serve either on their own or with whipped cream and berries. The meringues will keep in an airtight container for up to 2 weeks.

KYOTO TIRAMISU

Like many foreign dishes that have been adopted by the Japanese, tiramisu has been remodelled using green tea and sweet adzuki bean paste.

Serves 8–10

✳	✳	✳	✳	✳	✳	✳
4 eggs, separated	150g (5½oz) caster sugar	300g (10½oz) mascarpone cheese	1 tablespoon matcha (green tea powder), plus extra for dusting	36 small sponge finger biscuits	300g (10½oz) sweet adzuki bean paste	3 tablespoon sake

Whisk the egg whites in a large, clean stainless steel or copper mixing bowl using an electric hand whisk, until soft peaks form.

In a separate large bowl, whisk the egg yolks with the sugar using an electric hand whisk, until the mixture is light and fluffy and leaves a ribbon trail when dropped from the whisk. Add the mascarpone and blend until the mixture is smooth. Fold the egg whites into the mascarpone mixture.

Sift the matcha into a medium-sized bowl and whisk in 200ml (7fl oz) of warm water, little by little. Dip half the biscuits, enough to cover the base of a 6–7cm (2½–2¾in) deep, 25cm (10in) square dish (about 2 litre/3½ pint capacity), into the tea – they should be fairly well soaked but not so much that they break up. Arrange in a tightly packed layer in the base of the dish.

Mix the adzuki bean paste with the sake to soften. Spread half the bean paste mixture over the biscuit layer as evenly as possible using the back of a spoon. Then spread half the mascarpone mixture over the adzuki layer. Add another layer of soaked biscuits and then another layer of the remaining adzuki bean paste and mascarpone, smoothing the top layer neatly. Put about a teaspoon of matcha in a small sieve and dust over the top just before serving.

Serve in small portions as this is a very rich dessert.

BASICS

DASHI – THE INVISIBLE FOUNDATION OF JAPANESE CUISINE

There is a saying in Japan that food is to be eaten with the eye – meaning that it should not only taste good but also be a feast for the eye. But there is one element that is not apparent to the eye called "dashi", the stock that forms the foundation of, and invisibly penetrates, much of Japanese cuisine.

Unlike Western stock where simple ingredients are simmered for a long time, dashi is instead a selection of carefully prepared ingredients that are briefly soaked in water or heated so as to extract nothing other than the very essence of the ingredients' flavour. Indeed, the correct term of making dashi is "to draw" it.

Dashi most commonly uses a combination of konbu, kelp and *katsuobushi* (dried bonito flakes), but other ingredients such as dried shiitake mushrooms or niboshi (small dried fish) are also used. In general, there are two types – *ichiban* (primary) dashi and *niban* (secondary) dashi.

In Japanese cuisine, dashi provides a subtle undertone to almost all savoury foods. It is not an overstatement to say that dashi is at the heart of Japanese cuisine, not because of the prominence of its own flavour, but because of the way it enhances and harmonises the flavours of other ingredients. The quintessence of Japanese cooking is not to change or to impose but to enhance and harmonise the taste and flavour of natural ingredients.

Before the age of instant seasonings, almost every Japanese meal began with making fresh dashi from scratch. Today, most Japanese home cooks rely on instant dashi, packaged granules that dissolve in hot water, generically called *dashi-no-moto*, and you probably will turn to this instant method also. Although some are excellent, nothing compares with the subtle flavour and delicate aroma of freshly made dashi. I believe it is important that you understand the traditional method not least because it is neither difficult nor time consuming.

PRIMARY DASHI [ICHIBAN DASHI]

Ichiban dashi is delicate tasting with an exquisite aroma. It is mainly used in clear consommé-type soups for its fragrance and as a stock base for simmered and steamed dishes. Well-made *ichiban* dashi is so delicious and fragrant that it is good enough to drink on its own. *Ichiban* dashi does not keep well as the aroma fades if left to stand, so make it just before it is needed. It takes less than 15 minutes.

Makes about 1 litre (1¾ pints)

❋	❋	❋
1 postcard-size piece of dried kelp	1 litre soft mineral water or filtered tap water, left to stand overnight or boiled then cooled to disperse any chloric smell	30g *katsuobushi* (dried bonito flakes)

Place the kelp and water in a saucepan and gently heat, uncovered, to just below boiling point where tiny bubbles begin to appear – this should take 10–12 minutes. Don't allow the water to reach a full boil, and if necessary add 60ml (4 tablespoons) of cold water to keep the temperature steady. Kelp emits a strong odour and will discolour the water if boiled, so remove it immediately when bubbles start to appear and set aside. Bring the water to a rapid boil briefly and add 60ml (4 tablespoons) of cold water and turn off the heat. Add the bonito flakes but do not stir and allow the flakes to settle naturally on the bottom of the pan. Skim off any scum that has risen to the surface. Strain the dashi through a muslin-lined sieve and use immediately. Reserve the bonito flakes and kelp for Secondary Dashi (*see* page 144).

NOTE
In this book where dashi is listed as an ingredient, it refers to primary dashi unless otherwise stated.

SECONDARY DASHI [NIBAN-DASHI]

While primary dashi holds the namesake prime position because of its fragrance, subtle flavour and clarity, secondary dashi is versatile as a basic seasoning for many dishes including soups, noodle broths, cooking stock for vegetables, dipping sauces and salad dressings.

Makes about 1 litre (1¾ pints)

✳	✳	✳
katsuobushi, (dried bonito flakes), and kelp, reserved from Primary Dashi (*see* page 145 or Tip below)	1.5 litres (2¾ pints) soft mineral water, or tap water, left to stand overnight or boiled then cooled to disperse any chloric smell	15g (½oz) *katsuobushi* (dried bonito flakes)

Put the reserved bonito flakes and kelp in a large saucepan with the water and heat gently, uncovered, until just below boiling point when tiny bubbles begin to appear. Reduce the heat and simmer gently for 15–20 minutes, until the liquid has reduced by about one third.

Add the dried bonito flakes and immediately remove from the heat. Allow a few minutes for the flakes to settle at the bottom of the pan, then strain through a muslin-lined sieve and wring thoroughly to squeeze out every drop.

Unlike its older brother, secondary dashi can be stored in the refrigerator for up to 2 days or frozen for up to 3 months in an airtight container.

COOK'S TIP

If you just want to make secondary dashi alone from fresh, put a postcard-sized piece of dried kelp, 30g (1oz) of *katsuobushi* and 1.5 litres (2¾ pints) of cold water in a saucepan, and heat gently over a medium heat. Reduce the heat when small bubbles begin to appear and try to maintain the water temperature at a steady simmer for 4–5 minutes (add 60ml/4 tablespoons of cold water if necessary to keep the temperature steady). Strain through a muslin-lined sieve and the dashi is ready for use.

WATER DASHI [MIZU-DASHI]

Since the flavour and nutrients of kelp infuse water, it is actually not necessary to heat it to make dashi. Soaking for around 8 hours yields a delicious dashi. Because of the simplicity of the method, it is of paramount importance to choose the best-quality kelp possible – look out for thick, wide (no less than 15cm/6in across) leaves, in dark, rich amber with whitish powder encrusting the surface. Also the quality of water is important – if possible use soft mineral water, such as Welsh spring water or Volvic. Do not leave the kelp soaking for more than 8 hours because in addition to the glutamate which gives the most umami, other unwanted substances like alginic acid and minerals also seep out and discolour the water and the water make it glutinous. Good-quality kelp can be reused up to three times for this method.

Makes 1 litre (1¾ pints)

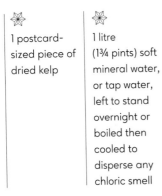

✳	✳
1 postcard-sized piece of dried kelp	1 litre (1¾ pints) soft mineral water, or tap water, left to stand overnight or boiled then cooled to disperse any chloric smell

Wipe the kelp lightly with a clean damp cloth. Fill a large glass bowl with the water and add the kelp. Leave it to stand and soak at room temperature for 8 hours. Transfer to a glass container with a lid and keep in the refrigerator for up to 10 hours. If freezing, use an ice-cube tray and cover with clingfilm or transfer the frozen cubes into a reusable ziplock bag and use within a month.

VEGETARIAN DASHI [SHŌJIN-DASHI]

Shōjin-dashi is a fish-free stock suitable for any vegetarian dishes and features widely in the Shōjin cuisine – Buddhist vegetarian cooking. It can be made with many varieties of dried vegetables such as dried gourd strips, dried soybeans, and *kiriboshi daikon* (dried daikon), but the most popular combination is dried shiitake mushrooms and kelp. While water dashi is delicate and delicious, for some it lacks in depth, but with an addition of dried shiitake mushrooms this vegetarian dashi has a fuller flavour.

Makes 1.2 litres (2 pints)

✤	✤	✤
3–4 dried shiitake mushrooms	1 postcard-sized piece of dried kelp	1 litre (1¾ pints) soft mineral water, or tap water, left to stand overnight or boiled then cooled to disperse any chloric smell

Place the mushrooms in a bowl, pour 200ml (7fl oz) of boiling water over and leave for 10–15 minutes to soak.

Meanwhile, put the kelp in a saucepan with the mineral or tap water and heat over a gentle heat until tiny bubbles begin to appear, which should take about 10–15 minutes. Remove the seaweed immediately, then turn off the heat.

Strain the shiitake soaking water through a fine mesh sieve and add to the pan. Combine. Strain the dashi through a sieve lined with kitchen paper and it is ready to use. This keeps in an airtight container in the refrigerator for up to 2–3 days.

TOFU DRESSING [SHIRO AEGOROMO]

A delicate, smooth dressing. Firm cotton tofu gives a slightly more pronounced taste and flavour than soft silken tofu. The key to success is to ensure the tofu is well drained (*see* page 100).

Makes about 130g (4½oz)

✳	✳	✳
100g (3½oz) firm cotton tofu	2 tablespoons white sesame paste or tahini	1 tablespoon white caster or granulated sugar

Roughly break up the tofu then wrap it in a cloth and tightly squeeze to drain (*see* page 100).

Put the tofu and sesame paste, sugar and 1 teaspoon of salt in a *suribachi*, a Japanese mortar, and blend well. Add 1 teaspoon of light soy sauce and stir well until it becomes a thick and smooth mixture. This dressing should be prepared just before it is needed.

WHITE SESAME DRESSING
[SHIRO-GOMA AEGOROMO]

This tastes like delicately roasted peanuts. Do not be tempted to add too much sugar –
it's used to give a rounded taste rather than to sweeten. Seemingly quite dry and coarse,
once mixed it will be just right.

Makes about 60ml (4 tablespoons)

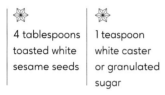

4 tablespoons toasted white sesame seeds	1 teaspoon white caster or granulated sugar

Put the toasted sesame seeds and sugar in a *suribachi*, a Japanese mortar, or use a
Western-style mortar, and grind to a coarse paste – leave some seeds still visible. Add
1 tablespoon of light soy sauce and mix well.

It's best to prepare this dressing as needed, although it will keep for up to a month,
refrigerated, in a ziplock plastic bag with as much air pressed out as possible.

SEASONED MISO [DENGAKU MISO]

As it is almost impossible to make dengaku miso toppings in small quantities, and as they keep well, refrigerated, for a few weeks, prepare them in advance and use as needed. For a nutty flavour, season the miso with toasted white or black sesame seeds. For a refreshing taste, season with grated rind of yuzu, lemon or lime. Alternatively, for a mild heat, season the miso with grated fresh ginger.

Serves 4

❄	❄	❄	❄	❄	❄	❄
200g (7oz) white or light-coloured miso	2 egg yolks	2 tablespoons sake	2 tablespoons mirin	2 tablespoons sugar	7 tablespoons Water Dashi or Vegetarian Dashi (*see* pages 146–147)	fragrant seasoning of your choice (*see* intro)

Combine the miso in a double saucepan with the egg yolks, sake, mirin and sugar. Put the pot over hot water and heat gently to keep the water simmering. Gradually add the dashi and stir until the mixture thickens and turns glossy. Quickly add one of the fragrant seasonings (*see* introduction) of your choice, varying the quantity according to taste, and mix well. Turn off the heat immediately.

ALL-PURPOSE NOODLE SAUCE

There are many ready-made noodle sauces available. Although they're a useful standby and many Japanese home cooks have them (including myself, I confess) homemade is much better and more economical. This keeps for up to 4 weeks, refrigerated, and can be used for simmered dishes and broths too.

Makes 1.3 litres (2¼ pints)

✳	✳	✳	✳	✳
2 postcard-sized pieces of dried kelp	3–4 dried shiitake mushrooms	200ml (7fl oz) mirin	100ml (3½fl oz) sake	30g (1oz) *katsuobushi* (dried bonito flakes)

Put the kelp, shiitake mushrooms and 1 litre (1¾ pints) of water in a large glass bowl and leave to stand in the fridge overnight.

The next day, put the mirin and sake in a large saucepan and bring to the boil for 2 minutes to burn off the alcohol. Add the kelp, mushrooms and soaking water to the pan and bring to the boil, then add 1½ teaspoons of sea salt and the dried bonito flakes. Bring it back to the boil again, reduce the heat to a simmer for 5–6 minutes, skimming off any scum that floats to the top, then add 50ml (2fl oz) of light soy sauce.

Remove from the heat and strain through a muslin-lined sieve. Set aside to cool to room temperature.

Transfer the sauce into a sterilized lidded glass jar. Store, refrigerated, for up to 4 weeks.

HOW TO USE
The above recipe gives a concentrated sauce and needs to be diluted according to different uses:

Noodle soup broth: 1 part sauce and 1 part water
Noodle pouring sauce: 3 parts sauce and 2 parts water
Noodle dipping sauce: 2 parts sauce and 1 part water

The above dilution proportions are a rough guide and you may adjust the seasoning to suit your taste.

SALT-SALMON [SHIOZAKE]

In Japan, salmon is almost always sold ready-salted and it is one of the most popular ingredients – it appears at traditional breakfast, in lunchboxes or even at a simple supper table.

Serves 4

600g (1lb 5oz)
salmon fillet,
skin on

Rub 1–2 tablespoons of sea salt all over both sides of the salmon fillet. Line a plate with a double layer of kitchen paper and place the fillet skin-side down. Loosely cover the fillet with kitchen paper and place in the fridge for 5 days, after which time you will have a rather stiff umami-packed fillet, ready to be portioned and grilled. Salt-salmon can be stored frozen for up to 4 weeks.

SALT-SALMON FLAKES

Serves 4

600g (1lb 5oz)	4 tablespoons
Salt-salmon	sake
(*see* above)	

Cut the salt-salmon fillet into 2–3 portions so that they fit snugly into a large saucepan and pour over just enough water to cover. Bring to the boil over a medium heat, reduce the heat and simmer for 10–12 minutes.

Remove the fish from the pan and transfer to a chopping board. When cool enough to handle, remove the skin and any bones. Scrape off the brown meat and, with your hands, roughly break up the fillets into smaller pieces.

Wipe the bottom of a saucepan with a clean damp cloth, then add the fish pieces with the sake and 2–3 tablespoons of light soy sauce. Cook over a gentle heat until most of the cooking juice has evaporated, stirring constantly. Do not let the flakes become too dry, stopping while they are still moist.

Remove from the heat and spread out on a large plate to cool down before storing in the refrigerator in sterilized jam jars. The flakes will keep, sealed, for up to 2 weeks.

TWO-FLAVOUR VINEGAR [NIHAI-ZU]

A vinegar to use with fish and seafood.

Makes about 250ml (9fl oz)

100ml (3½fl oz) rice vinegar

Put the rice vinegar in a bowl, add 2 tablespoons of dark soy sauce and 150ml (¼ pint) of water and mix together, then transfer to a sterilized glass jar and seal with a lid.

This keeps almost indefinitely, refrigerated.

THREE-FLAVOUR VINEGAR
[SANBAI-ZU]

This is arguably the most versatile vinegar mix that can be used for almost any food.

Makes about 300ml (½ pint)

| 100ml (3½fl oz) mirin | 100ml (3½fl oz) rice vinegar |

Put the mirin and rice vinegar in a saucepan with 2 tablespoons of dark soy sauce and 100ml (3½fl oz) of water and bring to the boil over a medium heat. Simmer for 1–2 minutes.

Remove from the heat and cool to room temperature. This keeps almost indefinitely refrigerated, in a sterilized glass jar sealed with a lid.

SESAME VINEGAR [GOMA-SU]

This is thicker and more highly aromatic than other vinegars – the nutty flavour of sesame seeds comes alive when they are toasted and ground.

Makes 200ml (7fl oz)

100g (3½oz) toasted white sesame seeds	1 tablespoon white caster or granulated sugar	100ml (3½fl oz) Two-flavour Vinegar or Three-flavour Vinegar (see page 156)

Put the toasted sesame seeds and sugar in a *suribachi*, a Japanese mortar, or use a Western-style mortar, and grind well until it becomes a smooth paste, and oil from the seeds begins to seep out. Stir in the vinegar and mix well.

This is best prepared as needed because the characteristic sesame aroma is lost quickly.

WASABI VINEGAR [WASABI-ZU]

A highly refreshing vinegar mix for wasabi fans.

Makes about 100ml (3½fl oz)

2 teaspoons wasabi powder	2 teaspoons mirin	100ml (3½fl oz) Two-flavour Vinegar or Three-flavour Vinegar (see page 156)

Mix the wasabi powder with the mirin, then add the vinegar. As wasabi quickly loses its aroma, prepare this just before it is needed.

SWEET VINEGAR [AMA-ZU]

This is sweet and mild and can be used to dress vegetables such as cabbage (*see page 70*). The amount of sugar may be varied according to personal taste.

Makes 300ml (½ pint)

✳	✳	✳
100ml (3½fl oz) mirin	2–3 tablespoons white caster or granulated sugar	100ml (3½fl oz) rice vinegar

Put the mirin and sugar in a small saucepan and bring to the boil over a medium heat. Simmer for 1–2 minutes to burn off the alcohol and dissolve the sugar.

Remove from the heat and let it cool down before adding the vinegar and 100ml (3½fl oz) of dark soy sauce; mix well.

Transfer the vinegar to a sterilized glass jar and seal with a lid. This keeps almost indefinitely, refrigerated.

CITRUS SOY VINEGAR [PONZU]

This is another highly versatile vinegar mix.

✳	✳	✳	✳
120ml (4fl oz) lemon, lime, tangerine or yuzu juice or a mixture	80ml (3fl oz) rice vinegar	10g (¼oz) *katsuobushi* (dried bonito flakes)	5cm (2in) square piece of dried kelp

Put all the ingredients in a large glass bowl, add 120ml (4fl oz) of dark soy sauce, stir to mix and then leave to stand for 24 hours to infuse.

Strain through muslin and transfer to a sterilized glass jar and seal with a lid. Although this keeps almost indefinitely, refrigerated, it is best to use it within 2–3 months.

SUSHI VINEGAR [SUSHI-SU]

Sushi vinegar is a blend of rice vinegar with sugar and salt. It is an all-important integral part of sushi making and gives otherwise plain cooked rice a subtle depth of flavour and sheen. There is no-set-in-stone recipe and the ratio differs according to different types of toppings; for strong flavoured ingredients, such as grilled eel or cured mackerel, the sweeter vinegar mix goes better, while raw fish and shellfish call for less sugar and slightly more salt.

There is a huge range of different formulas and each sushi bar jealously guards their secret recipe. But the most general guide is, using the dry weight of rice as the base measure, 10 per cent of vinegar, 5 per cent of sugar and 1 per cent of salt as shown below.

(Adjust the amount of sugar or salt as preferred)

200g (7oz) rice
220ml (7fl oz) water
20ml (4 teaspoons) rice vinegar
10g (¼oz) sugar
½ teaspoon salt

300g (10½oz) rice
330ml (11fl oz) water
30ml (2 tablespoons) rice vinegar
15g (½oz) sugar
½–1 teaspoon salt

400g (14oz) rice
440ml (16fl oz) water
40ml (3 tablespoons) rice vinegar
20g (¾oz) sugar
½–1 teaspoon salt

500g (1lb 2oz) rice
550ml (1 pint) water
50ml (2fl oz) rice vinegar
25g (1oz) sugar
1 teaspoon salt

It is easier to make up the vinegar in large quantities and have it ready. It keeps very well, refrigerated, for up to 3 months. The table below shows approximately the amount needed to season cooked rice.

200g (7oz) rice
400–420g (14–15oz) cooked rice
31/3 tablespoons sushi vinegar

300g (10½oz) rice
600–630g (1lb 5 oz–1lb 6oz) cooked rice
5 tablespoons sushi vinegar

400g (14oz) rice
800–840g (1lb 12 oz–1lb 14oz) cooked rice
6 tablespoons, plus 1 teaspoon sushi vinegar

500g (1lb 2 oz) rice
1–1.5kg (2lb 4 oz–3lb 5oz)
8½ tablespoons sushi vinegar

HOW TO PREPARE SUSHI RICE

Makes 800–840g (1lb 12oz–1lb 14oz)

400g (14oz) short-grain rice	1 postcard-sized piece of dried kelp	6 tablespoons plus 1 teaspoon sushi vinegar (*see* page 159)

Wash the rice under cold running water, drain and set aside for 30 minutes–1 hour to let it absorb the moisture.

Put the washed rice and 440ml (15½fl oz) of water in a heavy-based saucepan with a tight-fitting lid. Make some slashes in the kelp to release more flavour and place it on top of the rice, then wait for 10–15 minutes before turning on the heat. Cover, bring to the boil over a high heat and, when it just begins to boil, remove and discard the kelp. Reduce the heat to medium and continue cooking for 6–7 minutes, then reduce the heat to low and simmer for 12–15 minutes, or until steam stops escaping. Turn off the heat and leave it to steam, with a tea towel wrapped around the lid to stop condensation dripping down on the rice, for 10–15 minutes.

Moisten a *hangiri* (*see* Tip) to stop the rice from sticking. Spread the hot rice in a thin layer in the tub. Sprinkle the sushi vinegar over the rice, then, with a moistened rice paddle or a flat spatula, toss the rice using cut-and-turn strokes (the lateral motion separates and coats the grains without bruising or mashing) and at the same time cool it quickly by fanning. This is a bit tricky to do by yourself, so either get someone else to fan the rice or, if you are on your own, alternate tossing and fanning rather than juggling both.

Sushi rice is ready when it has cooled to room temperature and the grains are fluffy and glisteningly shiny. Try not to overdo this as the rice will become sticky and heavy. To keep sushi rice from drying out, cover it with a clean, damp cloth until needed, but use it up on the day it is prepared.

COOK'S TIP

A *hangiri* is a specially designed shallow wooden tub, made of Japanese cypress and hooped with copper. *Hangiri* are expensive, even in Japan, so you can use any wide, shallow, non-metallic tub instead.

HOW TO MAKE THIN OMELETTE

It is helpful if you have a rectangular Japanese omelette pan, but a regular pan (about 18cm/7in diameter) can be used instead. Just cut off the round edges once you have finished cooking.

Makes 8 omelettes

✳	✳	✳	✳
4 eggs	4 egg yolks	2 teaspoons white caster or granulated sugar	4 teaspoons cornflour mixed with 4 teaspoons cold water

Mix all the ingredients in a bowl with 1 teaspoon of salt and strain through a sieve.

Heat an 18cm (7in) omelette pan over a medium heat and oil lightly with vegetable oil. Wipe away any excess oil with a piece of kitchen paper. Pour in just enough egg mixture to thinly cover the surface of the pan. When the omelette surface begins to set, pick it up and turn it over with a chopstick, or a fork, to cook the other side. Don't let the omelette crisp or brown – it should remain golden yellow. Remove to a plate or board.

Repeat to make seven more omelettes. Keep the round shape if you are making *chakin-zushi* (*see* page 28) or cut off the round edges to make it a square if you are making *fukusa-zushi* (*see* page 28).

HOW TO COOK NOODLES

Outside of Japan you are most likely to come across noodles in the dried form, but the method of preparing noodles whether fresh or dried, is the same – it just takes slightly longer with dried noodles and when cooked they double in weight.

To cook 100g (3½oz) (a typical portion) of dried noodles, bring about 2 litres (3½ pints) of water to a rolling boil in a large saucepan. The saucepan must be big enough so that the noodles are not crowded and for the boiling water to circulate – just like cooking pasta.

Add the noodles gradually into the boiling water so that the water temperature does not suddenly drop. Stir gently to stop the noodles from sticking to the bottom of the pan. Let the water return to a full boil and when it froths up to the top and is about to spill over, add a cup of cold water – this is called *bikkuri-mizu*, "surprise water", and the purpose of this is to ensure even cooking. You may need to repeat this two or three times, depending on the dryness of the noodles.

To test, remove one strand of noodle and bite into it – the noodle should be the same colour throughout and cooked to the centre with no hard core, yet still quite firm. Test frequently to avoid overcooking.

Drain the noodles in a sieve and rinse under cold running water, rubbing vigorously with your hands to wash off surface starch, and then drain again.

To reheat the cooked noodles, simply place them in a sieve or a colander and plunge into a pot of boiling water for 10 seconds or so. Separate the strands by shaking the sieve in the water, then drain.

JAPANESE IN 7

HOW TO COOK PLAIN RICE

When I first came to England to attend a boarding school I had the humiliating experience of not knowing how to cook rice in an ordinary saucepan. Nowadays in Japan, almost every household, large or small, even single student lodgings, has an automatic rice cooker, I mumbled in protest. Since then I have relearnt the art of cooking rice in a saucepan.

In Japan, rice is measured in the traditional unit of 合, gō, (this is 180ml/6¼fl oz in volume or about 150g/5½oz dried weight). Allow about 70–80g (2½–3oz) uncooked rice per serving. Short-grain rice expands roughly double in weight when cooked.

To wash, put the rice in a large bowl, cover with cold water and stir quickly with your hands for about 30 seconds then drain immediately. Never let the rice stand in this first milky water – the milkiness comes from powdered bran and starch that should be washed away. Repeat the washing and changing water process until the water runs clear, this should take about 5 minutes. Do not skip this process as poorly washed rice is smelly and spoils quickly.

Let the rice stand in a colander for 30 minutes to drain. While standing, the rice will absorb moisture and expand in volume by about 20 per cent.

Choose a heavy, round, deep saucepan with a tight-fitting lid. A cast-iron enamelled saucepan of an appropriate size is ideal. Cooked in too large a pot, the rice will be dry, or even scorched, while if too small a pot is used, with not enough head-room, the rice becomes gluey.

It is rather difficult to prescribe an exact formula for the amount of water used in cooking rice because there are so many variables – where the rice was grown, in a flooded paddy (Asian origin) or dry field (US or European origin), whether the rice is newly harvested or it has been sitting on the shelf for some time, etc. As a general, but flexible, rule, use enough water to cover the rice by 2.5cm (1in).

To cook, place the pan, covered, over a medium heat and bring to just boiling. Turn the heat up to high and boil vigorously for 2–3 minutes: the starchy liquid will bubble up and steam will escape from under the lid. When the bubbling ceases and it goes quiet, reduce the heat to very low and cook for a further 8–10 minutes. All the time you must not lift the lid but learn to listen. Turn off the heat, still keeping the lid on, and leave to stand to steam for 10–15 minutes before lifting the lid.

Fluff the rice with a well-moistened wooden rice paddle or a flat spatula in a cut-and-turn motion. If you are not serving it straight away, stretch a tea towel under the lid to catch and stop condensation dropping back into the rice.

EQUIPMENT

If you have a reasonably well-equipped kitchen you shouldn't have to buy a great deal of extra items. A few improvisations may be necessary sometimes but such things are fun and should pose no discouragement to adventurous cooks. As the aim of this book is to get you started cooking Japanese food, I have taken a minimalist approach, so the following items are bare essentials. Most are available either in specialist shops or on the internet. In Japanese kitchens, knives are the most important utensil of all, and are covered in more detail on pages 170–171.

BAMBOO BASKETS [ZARU]
For draining, rinsing, salting, tossing and lots of other food preparation, Japanese cooks have traditionally used bamboo baskets of various sizes and shapes. Although metal and vinyl varieties more like Western colanders or sieves are available, there is something rather satisfying in using a traditional tool made of a natural material. And they make an attractive bread basket when not used for Japanese cooking.

BAMBOO ROLLING MAT [MAKI-SU]
Strips of bamboo are woven together into a mat with strong cotton string. It is used most commonly to make sushi rolls but also to shape soft ingredients, such as omelettes, and to press out excess moisture. The mat usually measures 25cm (10in) square. After using, carefully wash under tepid water without any detergent, and allow to dry completely before storing. These are widely available, even in supermarkets.

DROP-LID [OTOSHI-BUTA]
The drop-lid is an essential tool in preparing simmered dishes. It not only ensures even heat distribution, meaning flavours penetrate better into the ingredients, but also stops the cooking liquid from reaching a rapid boil, so preventing ingredients being tumbled about and damaged. Traditionally made of wood, it should be slightly smaller in diameter than the pan, so that it sits directly on top of the foods being simmered. Soak briefly before use to stop it sticking to foods.

GRATER [OROSHIGANE]
Traditional Japanese graters give much finer results than most Western equivalents. The best ones are tin-coated, double-sided copper graters that are used by professionals but they are expensive. The average home cooks use graters made of stainless steel, aluminium or ceramic, which give just as good results. Available online or from Japanese stores.

MANDOLINE SLICER
This is a recent addition to the Japanese kitchen and hence there is no traditional Japanese name for it although it is often known by the manufacturer's name of *benrīna*. It is an efficient tool for shredding and slicing large quantities of vegetables. These are available from kitchen shops.

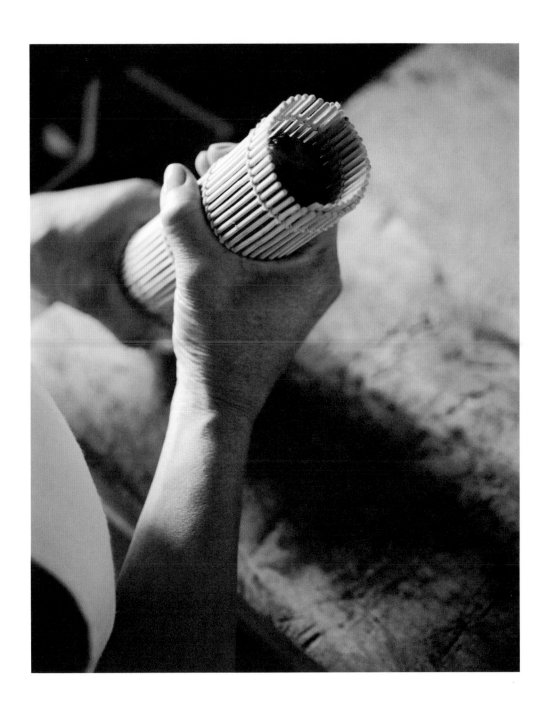

MORTAR [SURIBACHI] AND PESTLE [SURIKOGI]

The traditional Japanese mortar is a sturdy warm brown-coloured ceramic bowl, inside it is unglazed and textured with a combed pattern for a better grip. They come in various sizes from 14cm (5½in) in diameter to more than 30cm (12in) across but for home use, 23cm (9in) across is the most versatile. Hard wood from the Japanese pepper tree makes the best pestles but other wood such as paulownia or willow may be used. A pestle is sometimes sold together with a mortar but if buying separately choose one that is twice as long as the diameter of the mortar it is to be used with. To use, place the mortar on top of a damp cloth to stop it sliding while you work. Add the ingredient to be ground, gradually. Assuming you are right-handed, loosely cap the top of the pestle with your left hand and hold the pestle about halfway down the length with your right hand then rotate while pressing down at the same time. To clean a *suribachi*, you may need to use a stiff brush or the tip of a bamboo skewer once in a while to loosen any material stuck in the grooves. Available online or from Japanese stores.

OMELETTE PAN [TAMAGOYAKIKI]

Although it is possible to make a Japanese rolled omelette in an ordinary round omelette pan, having a rectangular pan makes it easy and reduces wastage. Professionals use heavy copper pans coated with tin but for home cooks, Teflon-coated non-stick ones are easier to use and maintain. To clean, wipe with oil-soaked kitchen paper then a clean cloth but never use an abrasive material or detergent. Available online or from Japanese stores.

A TRADITIONAL KITCHEN INHERITANCE

Not essential, but the most symbolic utensil in the Japanese kitchen is the small wooden rice paddle, *shamoji*. It represents domestic authority and when an older woman hands over her *shamoji* to her daughter-in-law, it symbolises her wish to pass over management of household affairs and is also an unspoken admission that the younger woman has finally become the mistress of the house.

KNIVES

Japanese chefs jealously guard their knives and would never allow anyone else to touch them. Japanese knives are in a different league from their Western counterparts. Like Samurai swords, they are forged of carbon steel and the blades are thicker and have only one cutting edge on the right. A single-edge blade cuts faster, much more accurately and cleanly than a double-edged one, and the thickness of the blade helps to separate each slice. There are 3 basic types of knives:

CLEAVER [DEBA-BŌCHŌ]

This sturdy, sharp pointed, carving knife is used to prepare fish and, to a lesser extent, poultry and meat. They come in different lengths but on average, measure 18–30cm (7–12in).

VEGETABLE KNIFE [USUBA-BŌCHŌ, NAKIRI-BŌCHŌ]

This single-edged knife is used for preparing vegetables. Although names and shapes differ slightly between Tokyo (rectangular) and Osaka (rounded top front) it does the same job of cutting, slicing, chopping and peeling. Japanese cooking involves a lot more preparation than Western cooking as the foods are all designed to be eaten with chopsticks. If you are going to invest in just one Japanese knife, a rounded top front vegetable knife is the one to buy.

SASHIMI KNIFE [SASHIMI-BŌCHŌ]

This long, slim-bladed knife is only used to slice boned fish fillets. There are two main shapes; in Osaka, the knife is pointed and called *yanagi-ba bōchō*, willow-leaf blade while in Tokyo, it has a square end and is called *tako-biki bōchō*, octopus slicer. Both come in various lengths ranging from 18cm (7in) to an impressive 40cm (16in). The reason for the long blade is in the way the entire length of the blade is used to slice sashimi. The Japanese dislike using the word *kiru*, cutting, because in the Samurai tradition, the word implies killing so instead, *hiku*, drawing or pulling, is used. You hold the knife pointing up at about a 45° angle and touch the fish with the lowest part (nearest to the handle) of the blade then bring down the blade, lightly pressing down and letting the weight of the knife itself do the work while drawing the knife towards you, using the entire length of the blade in all one action. This smooth one-stroke motion, no up-and-down or sawing movement, ensures each sashimi slice is cleanly cut.

CARBON STEEL vs. STAINLESS STEEL

There are two main materials for knives: carbon steel and stainless steel. While carbon steel knives are always the preferred choice of professionals, stainless-steel knives are popular in domestic kitchens. Most stainless-steel knives are softer than carbon steel knives and are easier to sharpen, but do not stay sharp as long. Carbon steel is harder than most stainless alloys but it can also be brittle, so pieces of the knife-edge can break off if it is not used correctly. Another disadvantage of carbon steel knives is that unless they are wiped dry before storing they can rust easily and quickly. Choosing a knife is highly personal, a knife that feels perfect in someone's hand, whether carbon or stainless steel, may not be the right choice for someone else. So if you want to invest in a knife, first assess how and what you mainly cook and how much maintenance you are prepared to devote to the knife. A good kitchen shop or, better still, a knife specialist, will be able to advise you on choosing a knife and also teach you how to sharpen and maintain the blade.

INDEX

ACKNOWLEDGEMENTS

My foremost thanks goes to Judith Hannam and my agent Clare Hulton.
My big special thanks to Emma Lee, the photographer, her assistant
Lizzie Mayson, prop stylist Lucy Attwater and, above all, Aya Nishimura,
the food stylist, and her assistants Sian Henley, Iona Blackshaw, Charlotte
O'Connell – for striding together to make this book happen. I also extend
my gratitude to the copy editor Anne Sheasby and designer Georgia Vaux.